FALCONS

PETER HEARN

MEN WHO TRAIN THE PARAS

GRUB STREET • LONDON

Published by Grub Street, The Basement, 10 Chivalry Road
London, SW11 1 HT

Copyright © 1995 Grub Street, London
Text copyright © Peter Hearn

British Library Cataloguing-in- Publication Data
A catalogue record is available on request from the British Library

ISBN 1 898697 19 1

Originated in Hong Kong by Modern Age Repro House

Printed and bound in Spain by Graficas Reunidas

Previous Aviation Books By The Author
PARACHUTIST
LONELY ON THE WING
FROM THE HIGH SKIES
SKY HIGH IRVIN
WHEN THE 'CHUTE WENT UP
(with Dolly Shepherd and Molly Sedgwick)
THE YORKSHIRE BIRDMAN
(with Harry Ward)
THE SKY PEOPLE
THE BARE KNUCKLE BREED
FLYING REBEL – The story of Louis Strange

To my fellow Parachute Jumping
Instructors past and present

CONTENTS

Air Chief Marshal Sir Roger Palin KCB OBE MA FRAeS FIPM

FOREWORD

Parachuting is not a well understood activity. In most people's mind it conjures a picture either of a sky full of airborne soldiers descending from somewhat rickety transport aircraft and gliders, or of a stack of free fallers weaving trails of coloured smoke across the sky before executing an accurate stand-up landing in front of a VIP group at some display. The Falcons, the Royal Air Force official parachuting display team, whose history this book sets out to tell, epitomise the latter. But there is much more to their story than display jumping, just as there is about the history of parachuting itself.

Few people know that parachuting had its origins in the 18th century when a Frenchman, Sebastian Lenormand , designed a domed canopy of linen and glued paper; or that today small groups of special forces can arrive in their target area undetected, by dropping at night from heights well above 20,000 ft. In fact there is a close connection between these very different aspects of parachuting, for it was the innovative enthusiasm of the early experimenters such as Lenormand which led directly from parachuting for showmanship to parachuting for sport, from which most advances were made in the development of jump equipment and aerial techniques, which in turn enabled the military application of parachuting to progress from the mass drops we associate with Arnhem and the Rhine crossings to the sophisticated methods used by the special forces of today. While sport parachuting is undoubtedly challenging and fun, it has thus been an essential foundation for both team display jumping and for the more esoteric forms of military parachuting.

The story of the Falcons encompasses all these themes, and the team has experienced its full measure of the thrills, the problems, the frustrations, and not least the very real dangers, during the first 35 years of its history.

Group Captain Peter Hearn, the author, has been closely involved with parachuting throughout his career in the Royal Air Force; in his early days as a Jump Instructor in the late 1950s he was one of the first team of four to be sent to France for free fall training; he commanded the Test Parachuting Trials Flight; he led the Falcons for a number of display seasons; throughout he enjoyed a close relationship with Special Forces parachuting. He is therefore well qualified to tell this story. This he does in engaging style, capturing the humour, dedication, courage and skill of the many characters involved: from the showmen Albert Berry and Leslie Irvin in the early part of this century, to Louis Strange, the RFC veteran who laid the foundation for the expansion of Britain's Airborne Forces which Winston Churchill ordered in 1941, and to today's Falcons who to a man embody the same characteristics of enthusiasm, adventurous enterprise and courage as their forbears.

This book fills a gap in our knowledge and provides a fitting tribute to the many who have committed their working lives to parachuting in all its forms, not a few of whom died in the process.

PREFACE

'How did it all begin?' is one of the questions asked of the young Falcon as he chats to people in the crowd after he has stepped so nonchalantly out of the sky in front of them. This book endeavours to give the answer.

Where possible I have told the story of this unique team through the recollections and in the words of the Falcons themselves. The account may seem overloaded with tales of mishap or near-mishap, but this should not suggest that show jumping is unduly hazardous. On the contrary: during thirty-five years of parachute display the Falcons have emphatically dismissed the 'dicing-with-death' image fostered by the old-time exhibition jumpers. But just as the commuter on the 7.50 recalls the occasional dramatic incident or wryly comic episode amongst otherwise routine travels by train, so the Falcon remembers best the more unusual of his journeys to work by parachute.

Many have contributed to this story, and my acknowledgements are extensive.

For illustrations I give credit to individuals where appropriate, and am grateful for their assistance - particularly that of Tony Betteridge who accompanied and photographed the Team during the late 1970s and early 1980s. Other photographs are from my own collection and from Falcons archives held at No. 1 Parachute Training School. Many of the latter were taken by a succession of free fall cameramen, namely: Terry Allen, Allan Rhind, Ray Willis, Bob Souter, Ty Barraclough, Pete Reynolds, Nigel Rogoff, Ali Wright, Jim Thompson, Greg McKenzie, Paul Floyd, Andy Wright, Steve Tucker and Colin Fallows. Some of the illustrations are included not for photographic excellence but for historical significance.

The leaders of the 1993 and 1994 Teams – Alex Jones and Steve Darling and their coach Rex Pritchard have been particularly helpful. For assistance and contributions to the narrative I thank them and other former Falcons: Ric Allison, Dave Armstrong, Tom Bown, Brian Clark Sutton, David Cobb, Rhys Cowsill, Geoff Diggle, Les Evans, Doug Fletcher, Joe France, Mervyn Green, Dave Griffiths, Chris Heathershaw, Alec Jackson, Johnny Johnston, Ali MacDonald, John Mace, Peter McCumiskey, Jake McLoughlin, Mike Milburn, Dave Paveley, Doug Peacock, Snowy Robertson, Mark Smith, Brian Stevenson, John Thirtle, Derek Warby, and Peter Watson. Peggy Williams and Val Greenland kindly gave me permission to quote their late husbands, Falcons both.

At No. 1 Parachute Training School, Wing Commanders John Cole and Ian Gardiner gave every assistance to the project, as did George Sizeland and Chris Thorn.

My thanks go to David J Bryan who as Managing Director of Sonic Communications Ltd. and an enthusiastic supporter of the Falcons, has helped with the launch of the book. Finally I am most grateful to Air Chief Marshal Sir Roger Palin, himself a former Airborne Soldier and long a firm supporter of the Falcons for providing such a gracious foreword to the book.

Right: Falcons approach the Royal Air Force Museum, Hendon, on one of their annual jumps.

CHAPTER ONE

FALCONS ARE FLYING

'Okay lads, listen in.'

The chatter and easy banter stop. They turn in their seats to face the Team Leader who stands by the blackboard.

'Today's demo ...'

The voice is crisp, matter-of-fact. The eleven men listening to it are attentive, quiet. They have heard the briefing sixty times already this season, but no two shows are the same. There is, in any case, no room for complacency in their trade, for it has much to do with the force of gravity, which is unforgiving. They are dressed uniformly in jump-suits of dark blue with red and white trimming. On their left breast they wear the brevet of the Royal Air Force Parachute Jumping Instructor (PJI). On their right is the red motif of a bird of prey with

wings spread, talons outstretched.

These are the FALCONS - the Parachute Display Team of the Royal Air Force.

'... The forecast is good. A little cloud at ten grand, but that should be clearing after mid-day, so there's a reasonable chance of a high one.'

He points to the figures on the board. 'Winds moderate, possibly gusting to fifteen on the deck by the time we jump. Direction south west, which is right along the crowd-line. Ideal ...'

The Team Leader trained as a teacher - a physical education specialist - and five years ago joined the RAF as a Physical Education Officer. He volunteered for training as a PJI, and after a year supervising the basic parachute training of Britain's airborne soldiers he was appointed to the Falcons. He spent a year as team manager, a

Above: Twenty minutes to go. The Team Leader copies the dropping instructions onto the briefing board.

second as deputy leader, and this season he leads the team himself.

'Aircraft is Hercules of 70 Squadron, with our usual crew. It's an airfield show, plenty of space, but we've got a VIP presentation as soon as we land which gives us forty-five seconds from last man down to line-up. That means accuracy takes precedence over everything else. The crosses will be right in front of the VIP enclosure. Let's all be there.

'Timings. We're opening the show with a P hour of thirteen thirty. Take off from here twelve forty, so emplane twelve fifteen. The Herc is landing to recover us to Waddington where we mount tomorrow's show, so there won't be a lot of time for the crowd after we've done the VIP bit. Questions so far?'

There are no questions. He nods to the Team Coach. 'Take it away, Flight.'

The Team Coach is a Flight Sergeant. He is the most experienced member of the Team. This will be his three-thousand-and-forty-ninth jump.

'Okay. As the boss says, we should get the high one. Four-way base as usual, and trackers - I want to see you back in with time to spare, and a clean stacked pull on my signal. If we have to come down for the mid show, it will be as normal. A low show is unlikely, but if we do come right down, let's see those exits cleanly spaced, and a definite movement away from the

centre line before you open.'

The Flight Sergeant joined the RAF fifteen years ago as a Physical Training Instructor, then qualified as a PJI. He has served at the Parachute Training School teaching Britain's paratroopers their basic skill; a previous tour with the Falcons as a sergeant; at Aldershot with the Parachute Regiment; and at Boscombe Down as a test jumper. His job as Team Coach is to instruct the team during the off-season training periods; supervise their performance throughout the display season; and during the shows to lead the Team onto the drop zone under their canopies.

'Nice and smartly into the stack, and let Andy come in at number six. If it's looking good, I'll call for the split, and probably one three-sixty spiral after that, but remember what the boss said - accuracy on the crosses is what we're after today. They'll be on the wind-line as usual, red for odds, yellow for evens. Straight into the line-up, and when the boss dismisses you, stuff-bag your rigs, stack them, and spend twenty minutes on the crowd-line. Colin - we'll have some stills of the canopy stack over the DZ.'

Colin is one of the team cameramen, who carry helmet-mounted still or cine or video cameras.

'Smokes ready, Jed...?'

'Smokes at the door, Flight.'

Each Team member has an administrative responsibility: photos, pyrotechnics, public relations, clothing and equipment, accommodation on tour, statistics .... They are sergeants, drawn from the trade of Physical Training Instructor. All are sportsmen, some with National honours. They look it.

'Any questions?'

Left: 'There it is...' From the ramp of the Hercules, above broken cloud, the Team Leader and Coach 'spot' the dropping zone on the down-wind run.

No questions.

'Back to you, boss.'

'Right. Standard emergency procedures,' says the Team Leader. 'Mark - complete malfunction of your main canopy …?'

The sergeant recites the actions he would take if his main parachute failed to open. He rattles them off as rapidly and surely as he would perform those actions were it happening for real... The others know them just as readily, but they listen. If he makes an unlikely mistake there will be laughter. There is no mistake.

'Okay. Let's make it another good one …'

On the airfield where the Falcons will open the air display in ninety minutes time, from a point just in front of the VIP enclosure there rises an orange meteorological balloon. Its flight is tracked by theodolite and recorded by two men wearing Falcon jump-suits. One is an officer, the Team Manager, now operating as Drop Zone Safety Officer. The other is a sergeant who would rather be jumping than manning the drop zone. From the drift of the balloon the officer calculates wind speeds and directions, and plots the upwind point where the jumpers should open their parachutes in relation to the two target crosses, already pegged to the grass, 20 metres apart and 30 metres from where the VIPs will be seated. On those seats the third member of the DZ party is placing copies of the Falcons annual brochure. He is a sergeant, a Survival Equipment Fitter attached to the Team and responsible for the serviceability and maintenance of their parachutes. Not for packing them though: they do that themselves.

Right: The Falcons get ready to go to work.

FALCONS

The high cloud, as forecast, is dispersing, the sun coming through to warm the gathering crowd. The wind is a steady ten knots, bringing to the DZ party the smell of aviation fuel and trampled grass and burgers; the sound of the crowd and a brass band and a kiddies roundabout.

A worried member of the organizing committee comes to ask the Team Manager for the second time if he is quite sure about the VIP procedure.

The Team Manager is quite sure ...

The Team Leader shares coffee with the captain of the Hercules before the parachutists board. They have been working together through the season, and the briefing and the exchange of information is precise and as comprehensive as it needs to be. Weather conditions, likely run-in track, drop heights, timings ...

'Two reporters and one photographer flying - all cleared, and on the manifest,' concludes the Leader.

'Okay. Loadie will keep an eye on them.'

The Team climb into the fuselage, carrying their parachutes, helmets, smoke canisters. Every piece of equipment has been checked before they emplane. They stow their gear on spare seats towards the rear of the aircraft, then move forward to more comfortable seating.

'Got the cards, Paul?'

The Team Manager checks his watch. Hour to go. Time for another balloon. Winds can be devious things. They sometimes seem to know when parachutists are coming. He takes the

Left: 'The first four have dived into space, already linked together ...' (page 23)

readings, converts them into a slightly revised opening point, and computes the track the canopies should follow from opening to landing. A smiling girl comes out from the crowd-line.

'How many tea tickets will you want for the Team?'

'Sorry. We won't be staying. The aircraft is picking the lads up within the hour.'

'What a shame ...'

The sergeant who would rather be jumping positions six smoke flares down-wind of the target crosses, and a set of flip-over panels with numbers on them on the up-wind side. The smoke will tell the jumpers the wind direction, the panels will show its surface speed. He will be calling it over the Sonic mini radio as well: each jumper has a receiver in his helmet. Now the sergeant tosses dry grass into the air to check that the crosses are still on the wind line. Technology is fine. So is dry grass.

Half an hour to go. Final balloon. Final calculations. Final dropping instructions ready to be passed through the aircraft captain to the Team Leader. Run in track, opening point, release point, wind speeds and directions up to 3,000 feet.

Along the barriers the crowd is thickening, humming with anticipation. The VIPs are being shown to their seats by the worried member of the organising committee.

'Good afternoon ladies and gentlemen,' comes the voice of the announcer over the loud speakers. 'Welcome to ...'

Twenty minutes to go. The Team Manager puts on the headphones of his Clansman radio; switches it on.

The Team Leader, listening through the

Above: ... while on either flank the trackers set off on their outbound course. Falcons are flying ... (page 23)

headphones built into his helmet, copies the drop instructions onto the briefing chart, converts them into symbols on the aerial photograph of the drop zone, marking prominently the release and opening points. The Team Coach listens too, and checks, and nods in confirmation. They are both fully kitted, ready to jump. For the next twenty minutes they will be checking the instructions, re-checking them, plotting that all-important release point, then guiding the aircraft onto it.

There are still whisps of cloud at 10,000 feet, but they will be able to see through them and are going for the high one.

The rest of the Team lounge quietly in their seats further forward, some reading the sports pages, others dozing, four playing bridge. One is talking to the journalists, who wonder that men can seem so unconcerned about jumping into two miles of space with their lives wrapped in a bundle on their back.

'Don't you ever get scared?'

They always ask that. 'If I got scared I wouldn't be doing it,' smiles the Falcon.

From the rear of the fuselage the Flight Sergeant is making rising motions with his hands. 'Twenty minutes, lads,' he shouts above the thrumming of the engines. 'Kit up ...'

Eyes open, newspapers are folded, cards are gathered and put away. They move down the slight sway of the fuselage to their equipment, not hurrying. They shrug their 'chutes onto their backs like familiar jackets, fasten the leg straps, then the chest strap, tighten them. They give their goggles a final rub, put their helmets on, then the smoke canisters, two on each ankle, mounted on metal brackets. Already through their helmet radios they can hear the sergeant on the ground calling out the surface wind speed. No problem ...

They check their altimeters, one attached to the chest strap, another worn on the left wrist. 12,000 feet, the altimeters say. The high one is on. That's good. They don't like it when cloud forces them down for the mid or the low show. Less impressive for those watching. Less fun for those jumping.

They have checked their 'chutes before emplaning, now they check them again, their own and each other's. The work of a PJI is a series of checks, a sequence of procedures that precede every jump. They are life assurance, and cost nothing but a little time.

The Team Leader waves them towards him. They gather close, leaning to study the map and the listed wind speeds. Their eyes feed the information into their minds. In free fall and under their canopies, the map and the winds will become reality. The Leader looks for questions. There aren't any. He writes ACCURACY! in large red letters on the board, and they nod, and grin.

Ten minutes to go.

The Leader signals to the Air Loadmaster, who nods back and presses a switch. The rear of the fuselage yawns, letting in a flood of sunlight and cold air and engine roar. The Leader and Coach move out onto the ramp to kneel at the side of it, looking down through the air-blast at the pattern of fields and woodland and villages linked by threads of road. Cloud like thin gauze

Right: The Team Coach spirals the Falcons towards their target.

covers it for a moment, then is gone, and there off to port is the airfield, runways stretched out like grey arms.

'Downwind. Five minutes,' the captain calls.

'Roger ...

They watch the airfield slide past, relating it to the map.

'Turning in for live run ...'

'Understand live run ...'

The aircraft eases round, onto the run-in track.

'On the nose,' the captain calls as the aircraft settles.

'I see it.'

Leader and Coach are leaning further into the cold slice of slipstream, looking forward and down, seeking and finding the wink of the ground flare right up against the curve of the concrete aprons and the crowd line, and the tiny

Below: The Sergeant, who would rather be jumping, radios the surface wind speed to the parachutists ...

Left: ... as the Team Coach leads them down to the showground.

thread of smoke showing the surface wind coming towards them, as it should be.

'All yours, Leader,' says the captain, as the airfield slides under the nose, out of his own line of sight.

'Roger … I have directional control.'

'Two minutes. DZ confirms clear to drop.'

'Understand clear drop.'

The Flight Sergeant turns to the Team, holding up two fingers. They make a final check of parachute pins and the safety lanyards on the smoke canisters, lower their goggles over their eyes, tighten their helmets, move onto the ramp. The reporters - safety-belted and moving up cautiously behind them - look nervous. The jumpers look like most other people going to work.

The Leader, face puckered in the slipstream, sights beyond the flare and the tiny target-crosses to the curve in the perimeter track which marks their opening point, and beyond that to the corner of the field over which they must leave the aircraft, and towards which he must now direct it.

'Ten left,' he calls.

'Ten left,' confirms the pilot. The aircraft eases round ten degrees on the compass.

The Team Coach is watching over the Leader's shoulder. He is more experienced at this business of guiding the aircraft onto the release point with nothing but a goggled eye, and will offer gentle corrections if necessary. It isn't necessary. The 'spot' is good.

'Five right …'

'Five right.'

Left: Falcons draw patterns in the sky with their split stack spiral.

On the ground, forty thousand faces are upturned, arms are pointing at the distant shape of the aircraft passing overhead, so high that it can't be heard above the expectant clamour of the crowd. A sergeant from RAF Brize Norton - home base for the Team - has taken over the commentary.

'… Any second now you will see the smoke trails as the Falcons leave the aircraft at 12,000 feet above the airfield. Four of those trails will be linked together in a central group, while on each side of them the rest of the team track outwards to demonstrate how man can fly in free fall …'

The Team Manager, whose responsibility it is to ensure that the ground and the air are clear for the drop, has a final look for turning propellors, stray helicopters, other things unfair to parachutists, sees none, checks the wind, then turns his head up to the distant Hercules. The track looks good …

The sergeant who would rather be jumping lights another smoke flare.

On the ramp, the Team Leader comes to his feet, looking directly downwards now as the runways and then the green fields unroll slowly beneath him.

'Red on …' he calls into the throat-mike.

The red light by the side of the ramp glows.

'Green on …'

As green replaces red, he turns to the goggled eyes watching him with what seems to be no more than mild curiosity, thrusts an expressive thumb into the air, disconnects his microphone-lead with a quick tug, and smoothly joins the stream of bodies hurling themselves from the ramp of the Hercules.

'Go ... go ... go ...' the Flight Sergeant is calling into the Sonic.

Within four seconds the reporters and the Air Loadmaster are alone in the fuselage.

Falcons are flying.

The first four have dived into space already linked together. Quickly they find their balance on the quickening rush of cold air. Clutching each other's sleeves, facing inwards, they grin through the wind-whip that flutters their jumpsuits and the loose flesh of their cheeks as it builds towards 120 mph - except the Team Coach, who has no time to grin, for his eyes are fixed on the living map below, checking their position above it, looking for the opening point, watching it come closer. It is his responsibility now to deliver the Team onto those pin-point crosses two miles below ...

Out on the flanks of the four-man base, four more orange smoke trails on each side are streaming outwards, dragged through the sky by the 'trackers', their arms close to their sides, palms down, legs almost together, bodies angled forwards, stomachs sucked in to give them the profile of human aerofoils. The deflection of airflow from their angled and curved surface drives them across the sky as they fall at speeds above 150 mph. Their eyes are on their altimeters. At 9,000 feet, after twenty seconds of flight, they lean back towards the drop zone, skidding through the air in 180 degree turns, then hunching again into their tracking positions, aiming themselves at the opening

Left: Leaving the side door of the Hercules for a 'low one', the first man already turning to look for the drop zone.

point over that curve in the peri-track, looking for the central smoke trail of the linked group, finding it, seeing it already breaking into four. The trackers sweep their arms forward to brake the momentum of their dive, then fly into their positions above and behind the Team Coach and his distinctive white smoke. Their right hands close over the toggles that will operate their parachutes, left hands reaching forward for balance. Their eyes are on the Flight Sergeant's left hand.

At first, seen from the ground, they were just threads of orange smoke leaving the aircraft, flying away from it in different directions. Then black specks became visible at the ends of the threads. Then the specks assumed the shapes of spreadeagled bodies plummeting earthwards as the smoke trails converged again.

Suddenly there are streaming flutters of red, white and blue above the bodies, and the blossoming of rectangular-shaped parachutes.

The Team Manager counts them.

'DZ control to Hercules, we have twelve good canopies.'

'Roger DZ ...' The captain acknowledges. He likes to know they have twelve good canopies. He banks the aircraft into its own descent pattern.

The Team had watched the Flight Sergeant's hand signal, had yanked their release toggles as one, and had felt the comforting wrench of a deploying 'chute and the tightening of the harness as it took the weight of their bodies. A quick glance to confirm that the canopy is all there in good flying order, then immediately they are easing down one of the two steering toggles to turn inwards, looking for

their place in the stack of converging canopies, at the same time tugging on the lanyard to set off another canister, getting an acrid whiff of someone else's smoke as they fly through his trail.

Now, adjusting forward speed and rate of descent of the high performance aerofoil 'chutes, they ease into position to form a tiered stack of canopies, close but not touching. The Flight Sergeant is the low man. He turns upwind to gather any stragglers into the stack, and when the Team has built above him, leads them round in a gentle turn to face the landing area. Eyes of experience assess the wind, the drift line, the zig-zag approach he must make to bring the Team onto those two crosses in front of the bank of upturned faces.

'Surface wind eight knots, gusting twelve' says a voice in his ear, and in the ears of the others gathered above him. It is the voice of the sergeant on the ground who would rather be jumping than reading off the wind speeds from a hand-held anemometer.

The Team Coach confirms the wind speed, checks the altitude, calls for smoke, pulls the lanyard to set off his own.

'How's it looking, Andy?' he asks his number six, the next most experienced man in the Team.

'Looking good Flight. Everyone in.'

'Okay. Going for it. Split stack ... Split stack ... NOW ...'

The six lower canopies swing out to the right, six upper to the left, painting twin swirls of orange smoke against the blue sky, then converging again into the single stack. There is a

Right: Falcons come home to roost.
(Photo by Tony Betteridge)

ripple of applause along the crowd-line. First time most of them have seen this done ... aerobatics with parachutes. 'That's amazing ...!' says the commentator, which isn't in his script.

As soon as the Team is gathered above him again, the Flight Sergeant calls a full stack spiral at 1,000 feet. Round they dance, all twelve together. Then he leads his flock downwind in a steady, curving run. As they follow him through a zig-zag of base legs then line up to land into wind like any flying machine, they become individuals again, each responsible for his final approach, each looking for his target, each coming in fast over the smoke flare, seeing the blurr of grass and the crosses looming, then cutting the forward speed with full depression of the toggles to bring the flying wing close to stalling point. Like giant birds settling to the ground on outstretched wings they step down out of the sky onto soft grass. Immediately they look for and dodge the others coming in behind them. Some land on the crosses, all are close. Applause comes to them as they take off their helmets.

They slip out of their harnesses and remove the dying smoke canisters from their ankles - careful to keep them away from the nylon 'chutes - then double towards the Team Leader, to form line behind him as he faces the crowd. He doesn't look for them. He knows they'll be there. The Committee member who is no longer worried leads the Very Important Personage towards them. The Team Leader calls the Falcons to attention and salutes the VIP and the crowd. With perfect timing the

Left: Two Falcons buddying .

Hercules that dropped them roars past close behind the Team and 150 feet above the ground.

'Ladies and gentlemen - the Royal Air Force Falcons ....' concludes the commentator.

The VIP congratulates the Leader, who then escorts her along the line. She smiles, shakes hands, chats to several. She is impressed by the calm assurance of these young men who have just fallen two miles.

The Leader salutes again as the VIP leaves, and when she has reached the enclosure, he turns about, and dismisses the Team. There is the roar of a Tornado jet making a low pass over the airfield to commence the next item on the display programme.

The Team Manager is packing the radio. The sergeant who would rather have jumped folds the target crosses. The jumpers bundle their 'chutes.

'Nice one ....'

'Not bad ...'

'One or two ragged landings,' says the Flight Sergeant. It is not his job to be entirely satisfied.

Kit stacked, they make for the crowd-line. They smile, sign autographs on programmes, on Team brochures, on backs of envelopes. And with modesty and easy confidence they answer the flow of questions ...

'How fast do you fall...?'

'What's it feel like ...?'

'How do you steer your body while you're falling ...?'

'Don't your feet catch fire from those smoke things ...?'

'What if your 'chute doesn't open ...?'

'How did it all begin ...'

Yes - how *did* it all begin ......?

CHAPTER TWO

FALCONS HERITAGE

The parachute was born of showmanship.

'There dyed one, some years since, who exceedingly diverted the King of Siam by leaping from the Hoop, supporting himself by two Umbrellas, the hands of which were firmly fixed to his Girdle,' wrote the French envoy at the Court of Siam in 1688. He added, '...the wind carry'd him accidentally sometimes to the Ground, sometimes on Trees and Houses, and sometimes into the River...'

Many a show jumper of today will vouch for the authenticity of this account, but alas - our Siamese tumbler and the even earlier umbrella-jumpers of Chinese legend remain figures of folklore rather than established fact. It is to Europe that we must look for our first acknowledged parachutist.

The concept of a 'fall-breaker' appears in the drawings of Leonardo Da Vinci and other Renaissance visionaries, but there is no suggestion that their theories were put into practice. The first to do that was Frenchman Sebastian Lenormand who in 1783 designed and made the forerunner of today's 'round' parachute. It had a domed canopy made of linen and glued paper, from which a wickerwork seat was suspended by cords attached to a strengthened periphery. He gave the name 'parachute' to the device, and tested it by dropping a puzzled cat from the Montpellier Observatory.

The balloon took to the air that year, and the

Right: The world's first acknowledged parachutist, André Jacques Garnerin, made the first descent seen in England in 1802 when he cut his semi-rigid parachute free from a hydrogen balloon, to land near St Pancras Church.

first to use it as a parachuting vehicle was aerial showman Pierre Blanchard. For the amusement of the populace he dropped an assortment of livestock in small baskets suspended beneath parachutes of silk. He was not inclined to follow them.

The first to put his own life in the basket was another Frenchman, André Jacques Garnerin. To attract the crowds and their cash to his ballooning exhibitions in Paris, Garnerin announced his intention to make a descent by parachute. On 22nd October 1797, he ascended from a thronged Parc de Monçeau in a wicker basket suspended beneath a parachute that to us would resemble in its un-opened state a shower-curtain made of cotton sail-cloth hung from a circular rail. This in turn was suspended from an un-manned hydrogen balloon. At some 2,000 feet above the astonished crowds he cut the parachute free. As it dropped away, the canopy filled with air, and beneath this umbrella-like structure André Jacques Garnerin came oscillating wildly but unharmed back to earth: the first parachutist.

Nobody was in a hurry to become the second. Garnerin himself repeated the venture only eight times in as many years - his third descent being the first seen in England when in 1803 he ascended from Audley Street and parachuted back to a riotous reception in fields close to where St Pancras Station now stands. So vicious were the oscillations of his almost impermeable canopy that he was ungratefully sick over the heads of those who bore him away in triumph.

For almost a century after Garnerin's first descent, parachuting remained an infrequent act, performed by a handful of intrepid men - and women, for the aerial showmen were quick to appreciate that the public pleasure in watching others at great hazard is intensified if the 'others' are young, pretty, and female. During this time the parachute served no scientific purpose. It was merely a showman's vehicle. Parachutes were self-made variations of the Garnerin 'umbrella' design, with canopies of cotton, linen, and occasionally silk, stiffened with ribs of bamboo or whalebone, still bearing their passenger in a suspended basket.

By the 1880s it was difficult to impress the crowds with traditional balloon ascents and parachute descents, despite their aura of impending catastrophe. A boost to aerial showmanship came in 1887 in the form of the 'limp' parachute. Gone were the ribs and stiffeners, the central tubes and pulleys, the basket. Instead, a simple round canopy would be suspended 'limp' beneath the balloon, its lines also fully extended with the jumper sitting on a trapeze bar at the end of them. When the 'chute was cut free, the canopy would be filled by the upward rush of air. Simple. Its inventor, balloonist Parc Van Tassel, was fortunately unencumbered by scientific qualification, which never has been a boon to parachute design.

When showman 'Professor' Tom Baldwin (most aeronautical showmen assumed the title of 'professor' or 'captain', and few begrudged it) brought an improved version of the limp parachute to England in 1888, his much publicised appearances at London's Alexandra Palace attracted great controversy in the national press, questions in Parliament, and the largest crowds that the 'Ally Pally' had seen for a long time.

A host of emulators took exhibition parachuting into a golden age, which lasted for twenty years.

Far left: Dolly Shepherd, the 'Edwardian Parachute Queen'. (Photo courtesy of Molly Sedgwick)

Left: Dolly is hauled aloft at Alexandra Palace beneath a hot-air balloon, clinging to the trapeze bar of her 'limp' parachute, similar to that pioneered in England by Tom Baldwin. (Photo courtesy of Molly Sedgwick)

Above: Dolly survived the hazards of early show-jumping to live to the age of ninety-six and to meet the Falcons when they parachuted onto the promenade at Eastbourne in 1983. Back row, L to R: Ali MacDonald, Nigel Rogoff, Jim Hughes, Rex Pritchard, Nick Oswald, Dave Wood, Brian Stevenson, Reg Bailey, Al Chaney, Chris Simpson. Front, L to R: Dave Griffiths, Ron Crawford, Dolly, Dave Hart, Mike Milburn.

Above: Airmen of the Parachute Development Unit who made parachute descents at the annual RAF Hendon Air Pageants during the late 1920s were the forerunners of the Falcons. They took to the air by standing out on the lower wing of a biplane bomber, pulling the ripcord, and being hauled into space as the 'chute deployed.

Prominent amongst the new generation of show jumpers were the ladies: Katchen Paulus in Germany, Dolly Shepherd in Britain, 'Tiny' Broadwick in America. It was a dangerous game. When Dolly Shepherd joined Auguste Gaudron in 1903, of the four others in his team, 'Professor' Smith, 'Captain' Fleet, and Violet Kavanagh would die on Britain's showgrounds. Dolly herself would suffer serious injury and be brushed by death several times during her nine years as a show-jumper, but would survive to meet the Falcons at the age of ninety-seven.

During this era, parachuting gained a reputation as an exciting spectacle, fraught with hazard, and practiced only by the most foolhardy of aeronauts. This association with danger and death, partly deserved, was also much encouraged by the showmen themselves. It was good for business.

On the other hand, the show jumpers were responsible for most of the advances in parachute technology up to the First World War - and much of the progress beyond it. They first stowed the parachute into a container attached to the balloon; later transferred the pack to the parachutist and gave him a harness; even added a ripcord, although it was designed to be pulled by static line rather than by hand. And inevitably, the first to parachute from an aeroplane was a showman - Captain Albert Berry. In April 1912, he packed his parachute into a cone of galvanised iron attached to the undercarriage of a Benoist 'pusher', and at 1500

feet over Jefferson Barracks near St Louis, grasped the trapeze bar that he still favoured, and launched himself from the flimsy biplane. He landed safely, repeated the performance at Kinnoch Field a few days later, then said he wouldn't do it again unless he was paid a damn sight more. Good for Albert Berry.

His jumps from aeroplanes and others that soon followed - all by showmen - attracted little interest to the life-saving potential of the parachute. Even when airmen stopped waving to each other in flight and began shooting instead, a combination of technical problems and official reluctance to resolve them denied Allied airmen the comfort of parachutes throughout the First World War. German fliers were equipped with showman Otto Heinecke's static-line operated parachute during the last few months of the conflict, and the crews of observation balloons on both side of the 'lines' used 'chutes adapted from those developed by the show jumpers.

Not until after the War were the technical difficulties of escape from an aircraft resolved. The basic problem was how to operate a parachute from a presumably disabled aeroplane without fouling the deploying lines and canopy. Early attempts to separate man and machine were fanciful, largely impractical, and sometimes fatal. What to us is the obvious answer of dropping free then operating the 'chute was not even considered, for it was firmly held by scientific, medical and aviation authority that to fall freely through the air was to suffocate and die, within seconds.

It took a former acrobat, circus performer and flier called Floyd Smith, and a Californian show jumper called Leslie 'Sky High' Irvin, to prove them wrong. Neither of them believed that scientific guff about passing out in free fall. Floyd Smith, as chief engineer of the US Army Aviation Service parachute test team at McCook Field, designed and made the first manually operated parachute, in which canopy and lines were deployed by the jumper pulling a 'ripcord', and Leslie Irvin was the first man to jump with it, at McCook Field on 19th April 1919. They revolutionised parachuting. The manually operated 'chute designed by Floyd Smith and subsequently manufactured by Leslie Irvin would within a decade be worn by most of the air forces of the world.

When, belatedly, the Royal Air Force was equipped with parachutes in 1926, a small team of airmen toured the operational airfields giving demonstration jumps from Vimy and Virginia biplane bombers. Before advancing to free fall drops of brief duration, initial descents were made by the simple process of standing on the lower wing, pulling the ripcord whilst clinging to the outer rear strut, and being hauled bodily into space by the deploying parachute. That team of spirited young parachutists combined demonstration and teaching with the testing of new parachute equipment, and also formed the nucleus of the display teams that gave public exhibitions of parachuting at the annual 'Air Day' at RAF Hendon. They were the fore-runners of today's Parachute Jumping Instructors, and of the Falcons.

Foremost among them were Corporals Dobbs and East. The latter in particular became one of the first 'skydivers' long before the term was coined. Through trial and error he found that by spreading out his limbs whilst falling in a face-down attitude he could stabilize his body against the airflow. He further discovered that by minor movements of arms and legs he could turn his free-falling body in a lateral plane. It was probably pre-occupation with the exhilaration of these early ventures in body flight that killed him, for in a demonstration drop from 5,000 feet at Biggin Hill in 1927 he failed to pull his ripcord until less than 200 feet from the ground and died before his streaming canopy could take its first breath. 'Brainy' Dobbs died two days later whilst 'balloon hopping' at London's Stag Lane aerodrome.

Whilst the manually operated parachute brought some respectability to parachuting as a life-saver, it conversely gave the show jumpers an ideal opportunity to tease the public with even more spectacular acts of death-defiance. The sight of a body actually falling freely from the skies and the inevitable will-he-or-won't-he-open-his-parachute-in-time reaction added piquancy to aerial display. Mostly the air-circus jumpers and the individual barnstormers jumped from low altitudes where folk could see them fall, and pulled their ripcords 'when they could see the daisies'. A few went higher in well publicised attempts on altitude records - Americans like Art Starnes, Harry Eibe, Joe Crane, Spud Manning, and John Tranum the Dane. Some of these merely tumbled their way down through the lonely sky for a minute or more. Others found - as Arthur East had done - that they could balance on that 120 mph rush of air. Spud Manning went further. He discovered and developed the basic techniques of body flight: lateral turns, back loops, vertical dive to increase speed, angled dive to track across the sky. It is all there in a 1934 copy of Popular Mechanics, where it lay hidden until others thought they had invented 'skydiving' in the 1950s.

In England, the best of the professional jumpers was Harry Ward who had learned the trade as an airman with that RAF 'demonstration team' before leaving the Service and joining Cobham's Air Circus. For five seasons Harry jumped twice a day seven days a week for the travelling circuses. For his last two seasons he jumped with home-made 'wings' in emulation of the American 'birdman' Clem Sohn. He survived the experience and is therefore less well known than Clem Sohn who died beneath the streaming tatters of 'chutes and wings before 30,000 people at Villacoublay. 'The only way for a jumper to make a big impression on the public,' Harry said, 'is to make a big impression in the ground'.

It was amongst the American professionals of the 1920s that parachuting set off in another direction - to create one of those parachuting threads that would later be pulled together in the formation of military display teams like the Falcons. In their search for novelty in aerial display, promotors invited professional jumpers to compete together in 'spot-landing' competitions. Those nearest to the 'spot' or able to land within a 'pay-out' circle would collect the cash prizes.

At the same time but for quite different purposes the sport was also being promoted in the Soviet Union. Soviet authority saw in parachuting the means of encouraging the qualities of individual resourcefulness and corporate spirit, whilst also providing a reserve of semi-trained personnel for the airborne forces it was at that time building. By 1935 the USSR claimed to have 115 state-run parachuting centres and 730 parachute towers. These initiatives - one commercial the other political - would jointly contribute to the rise of sport parachuting to international status in the 1950s.

Those airborne forces being developed by Russia in the 1930s provide another of the parachuting 'threads' that lead towards the Falcons.

Italy had been the first to consider seriously the delivery of combat troops by parachute, but only on a small scale, whereas by 1936 Russia was able to parachute 1500 men and supplies into the Red Army manoeuvres at Kiev. The drop was watched by foreign military observers. 'A bloody stupid way to go war' was the British reaction. The Germans thought otherwise, and under the acknowledged architect of airborne doctrine - General Kurt Student - they pioneered low-level delivery systems using static-line 'chutes from the Junkers-52 transport aircraft. Above all they encouraged a spirit of elitism that ever after would mark the paratroopers of all nations as warriors of distinction.

In 1940 Hitler unleashed these young 'hunters from the sky' on Western Europe. One of those impressed by the novelty and daring of this assault from the air was Winston Churchill, who almost immediately ordered the formation of a force of at least 5,000 British paratroops. At a time when the Germans seemed poised for invasion of Britain, the Chiefs Of Staff were more concerned with countering German airborne forces than with forming their own. In the face of apathy, inter-service rivalries, total lack of equipment, and almost complete ignorance of airborne delivery, it took the

The pull-off is demonstrated in close-up by circus-jumper Ivor Price, later to die on the showgrounds.

inspiring leadership of Royal Flying Corps veteran Squadron Leader Louis Strange - and his complete disregard of official channels - to create at Ringway the Parachute Training School that today is home for the Falcons.

To assist his nucleus of inexperienced 'instructors' he called in three former show-jumpers - Harry Ward, Bruce Williams and Bill Hire. Techniques were rudimentary. Aircraft and parachutes were adapted rather than made for the job. Should the main parachute fail, there was no reserve. Three men died during the first three months of training. They were brave men who went parachuting in 1940.

When in 1941 Winston Churchill ordered a vast expansion of Britain's airborne forces, it was on the foundations laid by Louis Strange and his pioneers that Wing Commander Maurice Newnham was able to build a training system that has remained largely unaltered to this day. Under his command the training of Britain's paratroops became entirely the responsibility of the Royal Air Force, who vested the task in its Physical Fitness Branch.

By the end of the Second World War they had trained at Ringway and at other schools in the Middle East and India, over sixty thousand British and Allied paratroops - 'men of the red beret' who carved out their battle honours at Tragino and Bruneval, in North Africa, Sicily, Normandy, Arnhem, and on the far bank of the Rhine. On the great airborne assaults and on the hundreds of moonlit sorties to drop agents and small groups of Special Air Service warriors, the PJIs flew with their trainees to despatch them into hostile skies. During those years of shared danger and adventure a great bond was forged between the PJI and the Paratrooper, which to

Above: Britain's first 'skydiver' was ill-fated Corporal Arthur East of RAF Henlow's Parachute Development Unit, pictured here when he joined the Royal Flying Corps in 1917.

Right: One of Arthur East's pupils, and Britain's most successful show-jumper during the 1930s, was Harry Ward, seen here coming to earth under his distinctive 'Russell Lobe' canopy when jumping for Cobham's Air Circus. (Photo courtesy of Harry Ward)

this present day has never been broken.

In the post-war decade the threads of show jumping, sport parachuting, and airborne delivery converged towards the creation of military parachute display teams.

When the airshows slowly re-appeared in the skies of America and Europe, the old time professional jumpers were mostly gone, and had taken their secrets and their skills with them. The new breed of show jumpers were mostly ex-paras in whom the excitement of the silken canopy still lurked. Nurtured on the static line, and now using surplus 'aircrew chutes' they

launched themselves with great enthusiasm and little skill into free fall display. In America too many died, and the hand of the Civil Aeronautics Administration fell heavily on free fall exhibition. In France it was an ex-SAS parachutist called Leo Valentin who - jumping with wooden 'batwings' - captured the air display headlines, none larger than when he too died at Speke airport with his splintered wings and tangled 'chute wrapped round him like a shroud. In Britain, four ex-PJIs - Ollie Owen, Johnny Rallings, John Fricker and Chuck Thompson - formed the Apex Group, motivated by parachuting itself rather than by

the few pennies it brought them at the shows. Ex-paratrooper Dumbo Willans earned a few more pennies by combining show jumping with parachute trials work, before giving himself to the teaching of others - for by the early 1950s, parachuting was re-emerging as a competitive sport and an adventurous recreation.

By 1950 the Russian and other Eastern Bloc parachuting centres had come back to life. France followed suit, calling upon show-jumping professionals to man ten State-sponsored centres. In 1951 Yugoslavia staged a 'World Parachuting Championships', involving delayed drops and 'spot landings'. Nearest to the 'spot' was an Italian, with a distance of 35 metres. In 1954 when the first official World Championships were staged, the British team included five hastily-trained PJIs. Even though they introduced the first 'blank-gore' steerable 'chute to the aviation world, they were outclassed. The competition involved accuracy jumps and one jump for 'style' which meant holding a stable position on a constant heading for fifteen seconds of free fall. Simple? Not in 1954...

Stability in free fall remained an uncertain achievement; body flight in the form of lateral turns, loops, angled dives, and variations in speed was a mystery known to few, and those few were beyond the 'iron curtain', or French. So to France in 1955 went American Jacques Istel, to learn the mystery and then to teach the skills to a first generation of American 'skydivers'. And to France too went a growing number of British jumpers, and as this growing band of young 'sport parachutists' became more adept, they began to appear at the air shows, marking the end of the full-time professional show jumper.

Amongst these sporting enthusiasts were a number of serving soldiers and airmen. Airborne forces had of course been drastically reduced in post-war years - in Britain to two Brigades, one of them Territorial. A similarly reduced Parachute Training School had moved from Ringway to Upper Heyford, thence to RAF Abingdon. Its role remained to train Britain's airborne soldiers in the basic techniques of static-line parachuting. Within the Services, the traditional airborne mind did not at first encourage its free fall enthusiasts. But younger, more adventurous spirits saw merit in it. In this age of vicious anti-aircraft weaponry, didn't high level delivery perhaps offer some advantage over vulnerable low-level dropping? Particularly for

small groups of specialists? Couldn't the skills of these sport and exhibition jumpers be harnessed to some military requirement? And quite apart from any tactical application, shouldn't the Armed Forces be encouraging this adventurous sport? And would the display to the public of this dramatic aerial activity perhaps have some recruiting and publicity value?

The threads were being pulled together by a few far-sighted military men. In America in 1958 Jacques Istel was asked to give instruction in free fall parachuting to a group of Army volunteers. And at No 1 Parachute Training School in 1959 four PJIs were sent to the French Military Parachute School at Pau for free fall training.

I was one of them.

Above: The first RAF Parachute Display Team drew on limited sport parachuting experience, embodied here in the Team that represented Britain in the first official World Parachuting Championships, held in 1954. On the left are Team Manager Dumbo Willans and GQ test jumper Arthur Harrison. The others were PJIs: Tommy Maloney, Norman Hoffman, Alf Card, 'Timber' Woods, Doddy Hay, Danny Sutton.

CHAPTER THREE

FALCON FATHERS

Our understanding of free fall in 1959 was still shrouded in the mystique of parachuting folklore.

As Parachute Jumping Instructors whose task was to teach airborne soldiers to leap into battle from low altitude, our world was that of the static line - that comforting length of webbing that instantly and automatically operates the jumper's parachute as he leaves the aircraft. What little we knew of free fall was fed by those PJIs who had competed in the 1954 World Championships. Their tales had much to do with 'spinning' and 'slow openings'. They and others had subsequently formed the nucleus of the Abingdon Parachute Club, free falling from a Tiger Moth at the Parachute Training School's drop zone at Weston-on-the-Green. There on a summer day in 1957 Flight Lieutenant Neil Perry dropped from 2,500 feet for a ten-second delay. He delayed much longer than that. Too long. When he pulled his ripcord he was less than four hundred feet and three seconds above the ground. His death closed the club, and rather coloured our attitude towards free fall.

So it was with a certain trepidation underlying our excitement, and a vague notion that if we spread our limbs and arched our backs in free fall we might attain this elusive thing called stability, that Flying Officer John Thirtle, Sergeants Alf Card and Tommy Maloney, and myself arrived at the Base École De Troupes Aeroportés at Pau in the summer of 1959, to be trained as the RAF's first 'official' free fall parachutists. Alf and Tommy had fallen free before, as members of that 1954 team. For John and myself it would be the first time.

Above: Over the Falcons' first home at RAF Abingdon, with Beverleys on the pans, PJIs make an early training drop using talcum powder to show their track.

My own remembrance of that first free fall was the feeling of utter nakedness that came from not wearing a static line. All else was tilted confusion ... Our training followed the standard French progression. It began with 3-second falls with the hand clutching the ripcord - jumps from which we learnt nothing other than that the 'chute actually worked. We progressed through 5-second delays to 10-seconds in the full spreadeagle position, then 15-second drops with a first attempt at lateral turns, and so on. The rate of progression was determined by individual ability. That ability was more mental than physical - and still is. The physical positioning of the body and the actions required of it during free fall are simple: less straightforward is the

mental capacity to order that position and those actions in an environment that is totally alien. The mind is too occupied with a unique blend of fear, exhilaration and disorientation to notice that one arm is not symmetrically aligned with its fellow, one shoulder dipped, one leg more bent than the other.

So at times we cartwheeled; at times we tumbled through the sky with flailing limbs; at times we spun. The spinning wasn't as bad as some had promised. It was like lying still at the centre of a revolving kaleidoscope of Pyreneean peaks, brown earth, and blue skies. It was as well, however, to try to stop the kaleidoscope before tearing at the ripcord.

We had no altimeters, no stopwatches. We counted off the seconds as we fell - 'Thousand-and-ONE, thousand-and-TWO, thousand-and-THREE ...' By 'Thousand-and-TWENTY' the counting had no doubt quickened a little. Then 'Tac!' as the ripcord was yanked. And then the pain ...! Those French parachutes were brutal. They had large, plain canopies which opened with immense violence before the rigging lines were extended, driving the breath from the lungs and the buckles into groin and shoulder. But nobody complained: buckle-bruises seemed a small price to pay for an open parachute. The deployment sequence also carried the danger of a flailing limb tangling with the canopy, so to lessen that possibility and also the better to absorb the opening-shock, arms and legs had to be gathered in and the body hunched before pulling the ripcord.

Free fall control came gradually. It came with more time in the sky; with a lessening of fear; with the consequent relaxation of body and mind; with increasing awareness of sensation and position; with a growing feel for the solidity of the air through which we fell. And control brought with it the sheer exhilaration of body flight. 'Knowledge Dispels Fear' is the formal motto of PTS: nowhere is this more apt than in free fall.

By the time we came to take a parting glass of champagne with our French instructors, that open door in the side of the Nord-Atlas was no longer a threat; it had become an invitation. And for our last 20-second jump over Pau, the Pyrenees kept quite still, smiling at us.

Below: The Parachute Training School Free Fall Display Team that jumped in Australia in 1959, seated in the Beverley before the drop at Amberley. L to R: Alf Card, Keith Teesdale, myself, John Thirtle, Pete Denley, Tommy Maloney.

We returned to PTS wearing our bruises like medals and with a quite undeserved reputation as experts.

We also returned to the luxury of a blank-gore canopy, packed in a deployment sleeve. The blank gore was only single, positioned in the rear of the canopy to give us a friendly nudge forwards of some 3 mph. 'Better than a kick up the arse,' said Tommy. But the sleeve! Now there was a humane piece of kit. It reversed the deployment sequence by holding the canopy until the rigging lines were fully extended, thus keeping it out of reach of straying limbs, and greatly reducing the opening shock.

Jake McLoughlin, then a sergeant PJI working

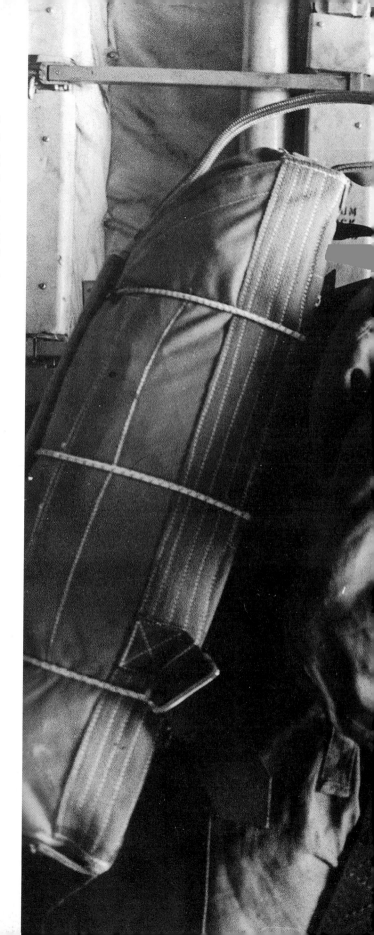

as a test parachutist at Boscombe Down and soon to join the 'Falcon Fathers', tells about the sleeve - and the state of British sport parachuting in the 1950s. The British team to compete in the 1958 World Championships in Czechoslovakia had been selected on the results of a one-jump British Championship held at Coventry airport in driving rain. Sue Burges won it with a score of 43 feet. Jake's 93 feet under a plain canopy gained him a place …

'I got to Bratislava by rail, equipped with my flat circular 'X' type canopy, an RAF flying suit, RAF boots, and a motor-cycle helmet. We got some high practice jumps and for some of the Brits it was their first ever attempt at a style sequence.

'The weather was perfect and one day I removed my shirt while packing my parachute on the grass. The Czech Gustav Kubek noticed the huge bruise marks round my armpits, and asked me what had caused them. He laughed when I told him it was the opening shock. He dragged me and my chute away to his club room and with a huge pair of scissors converted my canopy to a double-L blank-gore, complete with control lines. He then added a deployment sleeve, and showed me how to pack it.

'The first time I used it I was convinced I'd had a parachute failure, so smooth was the deceleration compared with the previous openings. Gone for ever was the seeing of stars when walloping my face on the reserve during terminal-velocity openings.

'Britain had its first deployment sleeve …!'

The British parachute companies had viewed

Right: The author giving dropping instructions to George Hill, Peter McCumiskey, and Stan Phipps.

Jake's sleeve and the double blank gore with misgiving. They had eventually adapted the sleeve, but told Jake at the time that the double-L canopy would never open.

'But I've been using it,' said Jake.

'It'll never open,' they repeated.

We also returned from France to instruments. Mounted in tiny pockets on top of the chest-type reserve parachute were a stopwatch and a miniature Cassella altimeter made for mountaineering. It was no doubt very good at telling keen-sighted climbers how high they were, but even if free fallers could see the tiny hand, it tended to lag some 500 feet behind them.

Thus equipped, we were ready to begin teaching other PJIs the skills that we had barely mastered ourselves, and to evaluate free fall as a means of clandestine airborne delivery. But not just yet ...

Already the potential of free fall as a crowd-puller and as a showcase for the values and spirit of the Royal Air Force had been appreciated. Before beginning our primary task we were to give a display, we were told.

'Whereabouts?' we asked.

'Australia ...'

Sergeants Pete Denley and Keith Teesdale, both with sport-jumping experience, were added to the French-trained foursome. We obtained white overalls designed for ground-crews attending VIP aircraft, stuck Union Jacks on our helmets, had our jabs, and were hurried off as part of the RAF representation at the Queensland Centenary celebrations. It was cheaper to send us to the other side of the world, someone had decided, than a team of aerobatic jet fighters.

Above: Stan Phipps leaves the Beverley in the 'classic' stable position which was taught at that time – arms and legs symmetrically spread, back arched, head up. Looks easier than it was ...

We hadn't really thought about displaying these uncertain skills of ours. Our minds were still much pre-occupied with the purely personal problems of stable fall, a clean 'pull', and a landing within reasonable walking distance of a cup of coffee. So we presented ourselves to Australia with a modesty that was not all assumed, but which seemed to endear us to the press and public, for the reception of the single display we gave at Amberley - north of Brisbane - was far more effusive than we deserved. The only concession that we made to showmanship was to cut slits in the bottoms of the leg-pockets of the white overalls, cover them with masking tape, cram the pockets with talcum powder then yank off the tape just before we jumped - to fill most of the Beverley and a small portion of the sky with visual sign of our presence.

Someone must have liked the show, for as soon as we had returned to Abingdon, John Thirtle was sent back with another hastily gathered team to jump again at Amberley, then to fly to New Zealand for a display to mark the opening of the new Wellington Airport. Winds of 30 mph cancelled that drop, but a display at Ohakea the following day was well received.

There was one injury during that trip. Sergeant 'Snowy' Robertson - a five-foot-six bundle of energy and wit whose parachuting would earn him the Air Force Medal and bar - jumped at the Amberley display …

'It was a poor drop and I wasn't going to make the impact point - probably a hundred yards short. I was being blown backwards into a swampy area, so I unclipped my reserve and loosened the strap that held it to the body so that I could see where I was going. As I came in backwards all I could see was water. I thought it was just surface water so I swung my legs to the rear to try for that show-off stand-up. The water happened to be about four foot deep with a foot of mud below that. Before my feet reached the mud the loosened reserve pack bounced off the surface, hit me under my left arm-pit, and out popped my shoulder. My feet were now stuck in the mud, the canopy was still inflated and pulling me back under the water, and I couldn't release my left leg-strap because of my dicky left arm. Every time I tried to lift my body I was pulled under again. Drowning, I decided that being a tall dwarf has its disadvantages. Fortunately Doc Johnson was DZ Medical Officer and being seven-foot tall ploughed through what to him was a puddle, and dragged me out. He did offer mouth-to-mouth, but I told him I'd rather go back and drown …'

Back at Abingdon we turned our attention from displays to the training of others and the improvement of our own skills.

Improvement - in skill and in equipment - was achieved largely through trial and error. Theory or the experience of others might make a suggestion, but the only way to test that suggestion was to go up and try it. This presented no problems in the development of skills, for what we did in free fall was beyond the sight and jurisdiction of others. So, alone in the skies over Weston-on-the-Green, we experimented with and taught ourselves the rudiments of body flight. We began to use the air pressure of some 35 lbs per square foot that acts against the spreadeagled body at its terminal velocity of 176 feet per second - achieved after ten seconds of fall. By slight adjustments of body position, and by offering inclined surfaces to that air flow, we learnt to turn laterally. We learnt to fall 'forwards' by tilting the body into a slightly head-down attitude with arms drawn back, legs closer together. The 'delta' position it was called. We also learnt - somewhat to our alarm at first - that a head-down dive considerably increased the speed of fall. We played with less productive but exhilarating manoeuvres such as barrel rolls and back somersaults - imprecisely called loops.

Improvements to equipment were not so easily

achieved. Quite rightly, the Services do not encourage the ad hoc trial-and-error process in the development of materials. They recognize a requirement; fund it; draw specifications; give formal approval to the resulting piece of kit; then create merry hell if the users start tampering with it - particularly in those days if the users were parachutists, for the official and scientific mind still considered jumpers, by the very nature of their calling, to be deficient in good sense. The same attitude that had told Floyd Smith and Leslie Irvin that free fall would suffocate them now told us that we couldn't remove the 'kicker boards' that provided a quite unnecessary base for the small extractor 'chute and which were also tearing holes in the canopies; that we couldn't have an extra blank gore for more steerability; that we couldn't attach the sleeves to the canopy so that we wouldn't have to walk across two manured fields to retrieve them after a jump. How did we know these things worked, and were good for us? Because at weekends we took our own converted American C-9 parachute rigs without kicker boards and with sleeves attached and with double-L blank gores out to the sporting drop zones where there were no restraints on 'trial' and no Boards Of Inquiry into 'error'.

Our debt to sport parachuting at that time was immense. It not only gave us as individuals an opportunity for experimentation, but provided a valuable source of information and guidance through its more advanced devotees - particularly those PJIs like Jake McLoughlin, 'Geordie' Charlton, Norman Hoffman, and

Right: The author, John Thirtle, Tommy Maloney, Doug Peacock, Snowy Robertson, Jake McLoughlin ... the first RAF Parachute Display Team.

We '...eventually found that with all six facing forwards, with tight harness–grips and a locking of legs as we stepped backwards we could survive the early turbulence below the Beverley until we were falling together as a stable group ...' (page 55)

Mike McCardle who had paid their way through the French civilian parachuting centres to form 'The British Skydivers Club', the foremost group of sport and display jumpers in the country.

The ultimate aim of the training and the trials and the improvements was not display jumping, however, but the capability to drop special forces from altitude, unobserved. This meant free falling with equipment, at night. At night? Not likely, said our scientific friends at Farnborough: not without some form of attitude indicator to tell us if we were upside down or rightside up, for as soon as we lost our horizons - they assured us - we would become fatally disorientated. We told them we didn't need instruments to tell us if that 120 mph airflow was blowing up our noses or up our backsides, and got on with it. Eventually six of us jumped from 7,000 feet at night with equipment-packs onto an unmarked DZ on Salisbury Plain and presented ourselves out of the darkness to a group of military observers. They had neither heard nor seen us arrive on the Plain, and seemed to have a sneaking suspicion that we hadn't jumped at all. However, a couple of weeks later eight men of the Special Air Service reported to Abingdon for the first British course in military free fall parachuting.

The training of those men and others, and the continued evaluation of equipment and procedures remained our primary roles, but throughout the summer of 1960 we were also called upon to give displays to visiting VIPs and at weekend air shows round the country.

Peter Williams, who would lead the 1962 Team with me, recalls one of those early displays. He took a group to RAF Dishforth, using the single-blank gore; talcum powder now packed into leg-bags; and those tiny Cassella altimeters. 'I wasn't over-experienced,' said Peter. 'This would be my eleventh free fall.'

He and his DZ Safety Officer, Pete McCumiskey, were met by the Station Commander and driven to a spot of grass between the control tower and an enormous hangar, and surrounded by a parked flock of Jet Provosts.

'That's where I want you to land!' said the Station Commander.

Peter demurred as politely as a Flying Officer should, pointing out that regulations required an area at least 400 yards by 400, and that the centre of the airfield was really the best place.

'Damn shame. Understood you chaps could land anywhere,' muttered the Group Captain.

Peter was adamant that it had to be the airfield, not the piece of grass alongside that vast hangar.

'Someone remarked,' recalled Peter, 'that we might as well drop at Scotch Corner for all the crowd would see of us.

'By the time we got airborne the cloud base was 2,800 feet and the drizzle steadily coming down. We plotted a run-in-track that took us towards the dreaded hangar with an opening point over the control tower for an estimated landing on the airfield. Standing in the door, enveloped in drizzle and cloud, I got the impression that flying on a given track in this lot was something of a lottery, but "Dad" Owen (pilot) seemed to know what he was doing. My altimeter told me we were either at 3,500 or 1,500 according to the milled edge that changed the height each time I moved. Splitting the difference seemed to give us a reasonable drop height. With chalk-bag zips open and everyone looking like adverts for McDougall's the green light invited us to depart the comfort and safety of "Dad's" aeroplane.

'In the five seconds of free fall I vaguely remember catching a glimpse of someone's chalk bag hurtling past me minus its owner. We opened in cloud, and as we emerged from it, instead of the airfield stretched out to receive us, immediately below and at what seemed to be about 500 feet was the upwind side of the dreaded hangar! We had been dropped way beyond our plotted release point. With feet up and using all of that 3 mph drive we skimmed over the hangar to arrive amidst Jet Provosts, people and concrete - on or alongside the Station Commander's piece of grass.

'Snowy Robertson was retrieving his canopy from the tail of a Jet Provost which was, to the buzzing crowd, all part of the game. I was picking myself up from the concrete when I was grabbed by a beaming Station Commander who pumped my hand and said, "That's gamesmanship for you Williams! Said you couldn't land here! Just having me on, eh ....!"'

In early 1961, we were told that we were to be formally recognised as the Royal Air Force Parachute Display Team. No additional instructors, however, would be established for the task: we would have to fit it in with our trials and our training roles. We were also told that as the official team of the RAF we would be jumping at the Farnborough Air Show in September.

Farnborough? With single-blank gores? On what would no doubt be a tiny DZ surrounded by expensive prototypes and expensive people?

'We need better parachutes,' we told authority.

But on the few occasions when authority had seen us jump we had always managed to land right in front of it, so it told us we were being ultra cautious. Authority wasn't jumping.

When we went to Farnborough in the early summer for our first practice drop on the airfield, a combination of wind-change and poor communications caused us all to land far short of the DZ. Snowy Robertson and Stan Phipps landed in the high-security compound, which they were forbidden to leave because they hadn't signed in. We blamed the 'chutes, and authority relented. New ones were ordered. They were still standard 28ft 'X' type canopies, but with twin blank gores connected by a lateral blank just above the periphery. A 'TU' cut, it was called in the sport parachuting world that had produced it. It doubled our forward drive to a heady 6 mph, thereby raising our margin for error over the opening point from 200 to 400 yards. It also increased our rate of descent to a bone-rattling crash.

We needed more than the improved 'chute. We still needed to be delivered onto that opening point by an accurate drop. In sport parachuting we had learnt to 'spot' ourselves by calculating opening point and release point from known or forecast winds, then directing the aircraft accordingly. In military free fall we weren't allowed to do that. When we dared to suggest it we were reminded brusquely that telling pilots which way to go was the job of a navigator, not a parachutist.

Fortunately, for the 1961 season and for Farnborough in particular we were assigned a special crew. John Leary as pilot and John Taylor

Above: Heading for Farnborough, 9,000 feet below.
The line up for the shows was L to R: John Thirtle, Jake McLoughlin, Doug Peacock, myself, Snowy Robertson, Tommy Maloney.

as navigator were to serve us well. To obtain more accurate dropping instructions we equipped the DZ party with theodolite and metereological balloons to read the winds up to opening height, then convert these and the forecast upper winds into run-in track, release point and opening point - all this to be passed to aircraft captain and Team Leader twenty minutes before drop time. These calculations on the ground were in the hands of our regular DZ NCO - Sergeant Ron Ellerbeck. Ron did more

in those days to get us onto our DZs than our parachutes did.

To familiarize ourselves with the shape and disturbingly small dimension of the Farnborough DZ, we marked a replica in white tape at Weston-on-the-Green. Anyone who missed it paid for the coffee.

As well as accurate landings, we also wanted to demonstrate at Farnborough our ability to move across the sky during free fall. We had now discovered the 'aerofoil track' position - more effective in terms of forward speed than the 'delta'. By sucking the belly in, slightly hunching the shoulders, and cupping the air in the hands in a revised 'delta' position, the body was turned into a human aerofoil, driven across the sky as it fell. Many believed that we couldn't do it, which wasn't surprising for we hadn't believed it ourselves just two years before. However, although we could move individually in free fall and could occasionally contrive a mild collision between two of us to pass a baton (John Thirtle and myself had been the first two British jumpers to achieve this exciting but non productive act earlier in the year, using a rolled-up sick-bag from the Beverley as our baton) we did not yet have the skills to fly into a linked formation. But if we couldn't fly accurately

towards each other, we could certainly fly away from each other. Thus John Thirtle came up with the idea of leaving the aircraft as a linked six, falling together for some fifteen seconds, then splitting and tracking away in different directions in an inverted bomb-burst.

Our first attempts were spectacularly unsuccessful. Six of us would step out of the freight-bay of the Beverley like an ungainly chorus-line to be cartwheeled and somersaulted and eventually flung apart in a flailing of limbs and boots. But we persevered with variations of the line-up and eventually found that with all six facing forwards, with tight harness-grips and a locking of legs as we stepped backwards, we could survive the early turbulence below the Beverley until we were falling together as a stable group. We would split after fifteen

Below: The 1964 Team. Standing L to R: Geordie Charlton, Julian Tasker, Brian Jones, Ron Mitchell, Team Leader Peter Williams, John Thirtle, Norman Hoffman, Ray Brettell, Jan Sparkes. Kneeling L to R: Dave Francombe, Paul Hewitt, Pete McCrink. The Argosy in the background was the drop-aircraft from 1962 until 1967.

seconds of grouped fall, then all track outwards for ten seconds before turning back and diving for the opening point.

To make the bomb burst and our track patterns clear to the audience below, we needed something more effective than talcum powder, and managed at last to persuade authority that we wouldn't set the aircraft on fire - nor ourselves, which concerned them far less - if we had smoke generators bracketed to our ankles. Also by now we had replaced those Cassella instruments with chest-mounted aviation altimeters with reassuringly large dials.

Six weeks before the Farnborough Show came the formal announcement. 'The Air Council have agreed that an RAF Parachute Display Team should be formed from selected members of No. 1 Parachute Training School, to take part under the general control of the RAF Participation Committee, in major parachute jumping competitions and air displays as an official team on RAF duty.'

So to Farnborough. Myself, John Thirtle, Doug Peacock, Snowy Robertson, Jake McLoughlin, Tommy Maloney. Mostly short men. 'The Big Six' they called us at PTS.

Cloud at 3,000 feet restricted us to low 'stick' jumps for the first three shows at Farnborough. But the two 'public days' at the end of the week saw clear skies and our first presentations of the bomb-burst. I wrote at the time:

'A loud "Way … Hayyyyyy!!" as we all step backwards into two miles of space. Big shape of the Beverley lifting away. Clinging tight as the line wavers and swings through sub-terminal air, then stabilised on the quickening flow. Grinning sideways at each other through the wind-whip, then looking at the living map of Farnborough

and Aldershot below, giving silent thanks to John Leary and John Taylor for putting us out in the right place, directly above the Farnham Road … Altimeters … 7,000 feet …. Letting go of the harnesses and diving away into the bomb-burst, turning back at 5,000 to track for the opening point over the Officers Mess, flaring out and pulling at 2,000 feet for that sudden transition from the 120 mph of free fall to the gentle sway of parachute flight … Loop the ripcord handle over one wrist, reach for the steering toggles, swing the 'chute towards the triangle of grass, the smoke flare, the target cross. Tack in over the public enclosures, across the runway at 800 feet, then the target looming satisfyingly large as you hook the canopy into wind and try for a showy stand-up landing even though you know the vertical shock of it under the "TU" is going to run up your spine and hit you on the base of the skull …. "Not bad," concedes Ron Ellerbeck.'

The immediate aims of free fall display by the RAF Team as presented at Farnborough 1961 have, with variations and vast improvements in application, remained good to this day. Firstly, the Team would present parachuting as spectacular and exciting - but safe. As Parachute Jumping Instructors responsible for the lives of others, safety was our credo, not the dicing-with-death image fostered by almost two hundred years of exhibition jumping. Secondly, the free fall aspect of the display would be based on movement across the sky. Thirdly, team and individual accuracy under the canopy would be part of the spectacle, as well as an obvious aspect of the 'parachuting is safe' approach.

The effectiveness of team accuracy - which perhaps we initially underestimated in favour of showing off in free fall - was brought home to us in early 1962 when for the first time the Team was invited to jump in France. We were to be one of four parachute displays at a major air pageant at Rouen. Our previous instructors from Pau would be appearing in a ten-man drop, and the French professional aces, Gil Delamere and Madame Violin, would be making solo jumps. We felt ourselves in awesome company, and hoped not to be overshadowed. The wind was an above-limits twenty knots on the surface, and a frightening forty at altitude. But the French would jump, we were told. So we tore up our own regulations ...

Our theodolite gave us an opening point almost a mile upwind of the target. The release point was almost off the map. But we had come to believe the theodolite and Ron Ellerbeck. We performed the bomb burst from 12,000 feet, and the angle from which the crowds saw it made the lateral movement even more impressive, but the greatest applause came when we skittered across the sky to crash into the turf all within a few yards of the target cross. Gil Delamere had jumped thirty minutes before and had only just arrived back from his landing several fields away. Thirty minutes after us the French paras came spilling from their Nord Atlas, opened their canopies above the airfield, and disappeared over the tops of the marquees behind the crowd. Madame Violin went in the same general direction shortly after. At an evening reception that was well awash with champagne we received an enormous trophy for the best performance at the Rouen Air Show 1962. The only way Gil Delamere could get his handsome smile in the papers was by posing with us. That was because we had been accurate, not because we had been clever in free fall.

We jumped again at Farnborough in 1962, this time from an Argosy. Because it was unsuitable for a linked exit, we devised an alternative way to show movement across the sky. As soon as we had the drop instructions I would draw on the map a 'flight plan' of perhaps two or three 'legs' which would trace a zig-zag of smoke trails through the air. It was great fun, streaking away towards the first turning point, whipping round onto the next leg of the route, then back into the opening point, assuming that the rest of the eight-man team were following me. Several years later Snowy Robertson said, 'You never thought anyone actually followed you on those crazy flights of yours, did you? No fear ... we just used to piss off for the opening point and leave you careering all over the sky by yourself ...'

After Farnborough 1962 I handed over the display team to Pete McCumiskey, and went with Squadron Leader Dick Mullins and Sergeants Dave Francombe and Paul Hewitt to learn lessons in Canada and the USA. At Orange in New England we saw Jacques Istel's commercial parachuting centre, the first to sell gravity to the American public. At Fort Bragg we jumped with the US Army parachute team, the talented Golden Knights, and joined the 82nd Airborne Team for a display onto an impressively small DZ at Winston Salem. In California I was introduced by the professional jumpers of Jim Hall's 'Paraventures Incorporated' to filming in free fall, and to the 'buddy system' of training whereby the pupil makes his first free fall from 12,000 feet under the physical control of an instructor - the

Above: When we established a free fall display team in Singapore in the mid 1960s, Snowy Robertson used to land on the athletics track, strip down to his running gear, and compete in the 400 metres.

fore-runner of today's Accelerated Free Fall Training system.

We came back brimming with ideas and recommendations, few of which were accepted. Authority either didn't like them, or couldn't afford them. Or didn't read the report.

Technical advance in particular remained a frustrating business. We had, for instance, long been worried by the tendency for the canopy to depart prematurely from its sleeve, and had recommended from our sporting experience the introduction of a particular form of 'mouth lock'. 'Not an acceptable modification' said engineer officers and others who weren't jumping with the thing. Then early in the 1963 season, 2,000 feet above the airfield at Perpignan, Pete McCumiskey yanked his ripcord ...

'I had the worst possible malfunction - complete bundle, rotating like mad. There was no way I could clear it. I pulled the reserve, and the inevitable happened - the rotation wrapped it round the main, and round me. Couldn't see a thing. I managed to claw some nylon away from my face and all I could see were the canopies of the rest of the team way up above me, so I knew I was going down really fast. I thought I'd had it. I was still trying to tear the thing loose, and suddenly the reserve must have caught some air, for it opened out with a bang. I had about 500 feet left. I landed on an aircraft dispersal, hard, but just glad to be alive.'

The parachutes were 'grounded' until mouth locks had been added.

Then towards the end of 1963 there came a major breakthrough in the procurement of parachutes for the Team. Authority was given for the purchase of the American 'Conquistador' parachute. This comprised the 'TU' blank gore that the Team was already using, but now in a low-porosity canopy which gave a more acceptable rate of descent, and directed more air through the drive apertures to increase forward speed. The canopies provided for the Team were in the pattern of the RAF's red, white and blue roundel. Even more important than the improvement in performance, safety, and appearance was the precedent that was set in buying custom-built 'sport parachuting' rigs for Service use.

One of the earliest appearances of the RAF colours was at Pau, when four members of the Display Team represented Great Britain in the inaugural parachuting competition of the Commission Internationale de Sportisme Militaire. John Thirtle led the team, with Sergeants 'Geordie' Charlton, Dave Francombe, and Brian Clark-Sutton …

'When the team got to Pau,' John recalls, 'We found it was a great festive occasion. All the other nations had their team managers, heads of delegations (including generals) and all sorts of hangers-on. We were just a wee team of four - one Flight Lieutenant and three NCOs. The French were a bit offended. However I reaped all the benefits; I was accorded all the privileges of Head of Delegation, team manager, team captain and Lord High Everything Else. I became a "Dignitary" of the Viguerie Royale De Jurancon - Mesté John Thirtle, that's me, and I still have my wine-tasting cup somewhere. There were seven precision jumps and three style. As a team we did better than half way but nothing to write home about. Fun, though …'

For that event, the team had been, of necessity, authorised to pack the Conquistadors - normal practice for sport jumpers, but until then much frowned upon within the RAF. It was another precedent; one that paved the way for eventual recognition by authority that parachutists were capable, after all, of packing their own 'chutes.

The frequency of displays at home and overseas increased throughout 1963 and 1964. France, Holland, Italy and Denmark appeared on the programme. The RAF Team was not the only military group now appearing at the shows. In America the US Army's Golden Knights was at the time the world's foremost team of display and competition parachutists. In England, our former pupils from 22 SAS had surpassed us as competition jumpers to fill the British Team in the 1962 World Championships, and were also fielding a display team - as were the Green Jackets and inevitably the Parachute Regiment with their Red Devils. These teams from the British Army - soon to be joined by a team from the Royal Marines - jumped at shows not as officially supported display teams but as representatives of their sport parachuting clubs.

Some of us had taken RAF show jumping with us on overseas tours. Snowy Robertson, Dai Hurford and myself - posted to the Far East Air Force - joined American and Thai jumpers in a display for the King of Thailand in 1963, and so formed the beginning of a FEAF Parachute Display Team. Cyprus-based PJIs would soon form a similar team for the Near East Air Force.

Although the Abingdon-based RAF Team enjoyed formal recognition and Service support, it remained for PTS a 'non-established task', with members drawn from its free-fall training and trials flights. In 1965 that was about to change.

CHAPTER FOUR

FALCONS SPREAD THEIR WINGS

Since the official recognition of the RAF Parachute Display Team in 1961, a succession of officers commanding PTS had been asking for that recognition to be backed by having men assigned to the job. In 1965, half the battle was won when authority was granted for one Flight Lieutenant and six NCOs to be established solely for display duties. To make the twelve-man team, additional instructors would still have to be drawn from other tasks. However, with a core of full-time display parachutists it became possible to encourage more professional attitudes towards show jumping. No one was better qualified to encourage them than John Thirtle, the Team's first 'established' leader.

With their new status it was time, thought John, that they had a more catchy name than The RAF Parachute Display Team. He asked for

suggestions. A bird, it was quickly agreed, should lend its name to the Team. A spirited, fast moving bird. A bird of prey. Hawks? Peregrines? Eagles? Falcons? They studied the dictionary definitions.

'... Bird with a long glide on extended pinions, falling extremely rapidly, much given to aerobatics and swift stooping flight ...' was the definition of the falcon.

Falcons they became.

The establishment of men for the job now allowed more time for team training. But parachute training during an English winter - and sometimes during an English summer - rarely offers the concentration of jumping that is the key to progression in free fall and canopy skills. Cloudless skies, moderate winds, soft and extensive drop zones - these are the conditions that skydivers seek. A desert? Why not …

In 1965, North Africa provided the desert. RAF Idris - close to Tripoli - was the first base for what was to become an annual series of overseas training detachments for the Falcons. For a fortnight in February and again in March the Team jumped up to three times a day onto a DZ at Azizya. Progression was rapid - except for John, who ruptured an achilles tendon during the second of the periods and had to hand over leadership of the Team to Stuart Cameron for the early part of the display season. He was back

Below: In 1965, the Falcons 'unveiled their new and at that time revolutionary parachute: the Para-Commander'. (Photo by Tony Betteridge)

in time to take the Falcons to Tehran to jump at the Iranian Air Force Day. There, for the first time they unveiled their new and at that time revolutionary parachute: the Para-Commander, to be known thereafter as the PC.

Initially conceived by Pierre Lemoigne for parascending, the design had quickly been adapted by American sport parachutists and had made its first appearance in international competition in 1964. The PC had an ultra-low-porosity canopy with an elliptically-shaped front skirt to take in air, which was then diverted through a series of driving apertures and steering slots to produce a controllable forward speed of 12 mph and a swift but stable turning capability. If such a complex canopy

Above: John Thirtle (right foreground) with his 1965 team equipped with the PCs. Others are L to R: Ralph Lee, Julian Tasker, Mick Geelan, Norman Pilling, Ray Brettell, Snowy Robertson, Brian Clark–Sutton, Ken Mapplebeck, David Jones, Jan Sparkes.

malfunctioned, it malfunctioned nastily, but this hazard was countered by a canopy-release system which enabled the parachutist to 'cut away' from it back into free fall and into clear air - in which to operate his reserve.

To the competition jumpers the PC would bring an almost monotonous succession of 'dead-centre' landings. To display teams it offered the potential for greater accuracy on smaller drop zones in higher winds.

Falcons were not fully equipped with the new 'chute until well into the 1966 season. Until then they used a mix of PCs and Conquistadors for their 12-man shows, and this mix was combined with a novel adaption of the movement-in-free-fall principle. At 12,000 feet, six men wearing the PCs would jump at the first release point, and would immediately start tracking in the same direction as the aircraft. A second sextet wearing the Conquistadors would jump ten seconds later, to track back towards the others. Hopefully, they and their smoke trails would cross at about 7,000 feet as the two groups continued to fly towards their separate opening points - the PCs' with their greater drive being opened further upwind of the target and higher than the Conquistadors. The concept

F
A
L
C
O
N
S

Top left: The team of Falcons who in 1966 at El Adem made the first British six-man link. Standing L to R: Geordie Charlton, Julian Tasker, David Jones, Ken Mapplebeck, Stuart Cameron, Brian Clark-Sutton. Seated is the Falcon who caught it on film, Terry Allen.

Bottom left: Geordie Charlton eases in to take the sixth position in the line.

Above: Terry Allen with the motorised Nikon for stills photography, Julian Tasker with the 16 mm cine camera.

of alternative display patterns if forced by cloud or other circumstances to drop from 'medium' or 'low' altitude was also formalised at this time.

John also made another significant advance. Peter Williams before him had laid the foundations for the adoption of 'spotting' by the parachutists themselves, but it was in John's time that the responsibility for the final guidance of the pilot to the release point and the call for the

'green on' was at last invested in the Team Leader. Authority didn't like the term 'spotting': it insisted on calling it 'side door guidance'. The jumpers didn't care what it was called.

Also by this time - mainly because there was no alternative to self-packing during overseas detachments - it was formally recognised that Falcons could pack their own 'chutes, under the supervision of a Safety Equipment Worker attached to the Team.

RAF El Adem outside Tobruk provided the venue for 1966 pre-season preparation. The results of this intensive training and of the improvements in equipment and procedures were seen in the series of displays given at home and abroad that year. No other parachute team in Western Europe was performing in such numbers with such precision, and to such enthusiastic receptions. Turin stands out in the memory of most of the 1966 Falcons. Brian Clark-Sutton recalls it:

'When we landed, all twelve of us round the cross - bang, bang, bang - all the people in the stands rose to their feet and started roaring and clapping, and I wondered what was happening because things were flying up in the air, then I realised they were all throwing their hats up, or whatever else they could lay their hands on. It went on for ages, and wherever we went that day, as soon as people saw our jump-suits with the badges on, they started clapping. It was embarrassing. Nice, though ...'

Brian Clark-Sutton was one of six Falcons who established a landmark in the Team's history during autumn training at El Adem that year. The days of individual 'baton passes' were over. Skydiving was now entering the era of more advanced 'relative work' in which groups of free fallers flew their bodies into linked formations. In the blue skies of California in 1964, American

Below: The Falcons' falcon 'Quinquaginta', with his handler Peter Davis. Ray Brettell to left, Geoff Greenland behind Peter, Joe Featherstone to the right.

skydivers had formed the first 6-man 'star' - in fact an inward-facing circle of linked bodies. In 1965 it was an 8-man. Now, in 1966 at El Adem the more proficient amongst the Falcons tried this new game. Four times they completed 3-man links, three times they put together a 4-man star. Then they tried for the six …

They deliberately planned a line-abreast formation, not appreciating at the time that although easier to achieve, a line would be more difficult to hold than a 'star'. Each man had his allotted place in the line. Stuart Cameron and Ken Mapplebeck were the first out of the twin doors of the Argosy. They slid across the slipstream to form a 2-man base within five seconds. David Jones flew in to take Stuart Cameron by the wrist, while Julian Tasker linked alongside Ken Mapplebeck. Geordie Charlton and Brian Clark-Sutton had the hardest job. As last men out of the aircraft they had to lose height and cover space to catch up with the others, then convert the speed of that dive into a steady lateral approach. Over-enthusiasm could take them past the slower falling foursome or into a heavy collision that would blow the formation apart. The linked four held the line with constant adjustments to their leg positions while first Brian then Geordie flew slowly but steadily into their places on the wings.

The Falcons were living up to their name: they were flying.

Even more significant than the British record for the first 6-man link was the capture of the achievement on film. Air-to-air photography by free falling cameramen had also been pioneered in Californian skies. In Britain, one of the first to mount a camera on his helmet was Charles Shea-Simonds, then a Lieutenant in the Parachute Regiment. When the Falcons went to El Adem in late 1966 he loaned them his motorised Nikon for stills photography, to be shot by Flight Sergeant Terry Allen and Brian Clark-Sutton. For cine filming, Julian Tasker carried either a helmet-mounted GSAP 16 mm camera or a new all-electric 16 mm Beulie. The aerial shots of the linked-6 taken by Terry Allen were good enough and certainly at that time sensational enough to capture the front page of the *Daily Telegraph*.

It was the beginning of an era during which the airborne camera would serve the dual role of publicising the Team in dramatic fashion, and of providing a valuable training aid.

It took time to build those early formations. The mid-60s were a transition period between the partially controlled movement of which we had been capable in 1960, and the swift precision of body flight yet to be achieved in competitive 'speed stars' and sequential relative work. To give themselves time in the air during which to form their link, the Team at El Adem jumped from heights in excess of the normal 12,000 feet. This required them to use oxygen. During the climb to altitude it was provided from the aircraft's central console. Just before jumping, parachutists would transfer to their own personal 'bottles', carried above the reserve 'chute. One such jump was made from 20,000 feet, but the additional equipment impeded body flight, especially for the already-laden cameramen. And who wanted to be hidden behind an oxygen-mask with all those cameras around …? So for subsequent attempts at formation-flying they came down to 16,000 feet where it was considered safe to 'pre-oxygenate' on the console, then disengage seconds before jumping.

The use of oxygen and the attempts to fly in close formation during free fall were not purely in the interests of show-jumping and publicity. The ability of a group to fall in close proximity from high altitude and to keep position with a free-dropped equipment-container was soon to become the basis of military free fall. Falcons would develop this technique, and it would be ex-Falcons who would teach it to Britain's special forces.

Falcons spread their wings over new horizons in 1967 when in addition to appearances throughout Europe they travelled west - to Canada, for six shows at the Abbotsford Air Show in Vancouver. Of Canada, one remarked, 'That's a bloody big wood down there. We've been flying over it for eight hours.'

In 1968 the Falcons performed for the first time before Her Majesty The Queen. The occasion was a suitably impressive air display at RAF Abingdon to mark the 50th anniversary of the Royal Air Force.

The Team Leader was Geoff Greenland, a Yorkshireman with a chirpy sense of humour but no time for nonsense - and not much worried about a bit of wind. And there was a bit of wind on the day of the Abingdon display. In fact, it was gusting well above limits. But this was a Royal show, and on Falcons' home ground too, so there was no question in Geoff's mind of scrubbing the drop.

The officer commanding PTS - first in line for official wrath should the drop go astray - did not share his Team Leader's confidence. People on the ground rarely do. As the aircraft turned onto its approach run for the airfield, with winds gusting to 20 knots, he sent a call for the drop to be abandoned. Geoff was in the open door, already 'spotting' the target as it moved immediately below, when the message to abort because of high winds was relayed to him through the aircraft captain. The message was clear enough, but 'Sorry skipper,' said Geoff over his intercom, 'Lots of static back here. I didn't quite get that. Green on, please Nav ....'

The navigator switched on the green light. Geoff disconnected his intercom before anyone could pass him more daft instructions, and led the Team out of the door. They landed well on target, nobody was hurt, and OC PTS was warmly congratulated on providing such a fine show.

Also present at the event was a real falcon - an Indian Lagger bird, given honorary non-jumping status as a member of the Team earlier that year. In recognition of the 50th Anniversary, he was named 'Quinquaginta'. Sensible people called him Fred. Fred would spend four years with his fellow Falcons, accompanying them to shows around the world, attracting more photographers than other Team members, and crapping on expensive carpets at official receptions.

Geoff Greenland had more than his fair share of poor weather during 1968. His deputy, Mervyn Green, remembers one such occasion .....

'It was the practise day for the Biggin Hill show, and me with all of twenty-four free fall jumps to my name. Gusty winds, raining, cloud base around 2,500. Was life on the Falcons always going to be as enjoyable as this, I wondered? We dropped far too far away from the airfield, and I just managed to clear the perimeter fence and landed safely after asking a startled spectator to kindly shift himself from beneath my size tens ... or words to that effect. Only half the Team had made the airfield. The more experienced hands had wisely decided not even to try for it, but to seek safer landing areas outside the fence. We eventually located them all, including Flight Sergeant Terry Allen, who was found sitting in someone's back garden having tea and biscuits.'

Conditions for the actual show were much the same, except that the winds were even stronger. 'We'll give it a go,' said Geoff.

off across the pans, being dragged on my backside. The next thing I knew was a sudden battering as the canopy and myself were whiplashed under the fuselage of an aircraft. When I got out, my helmet was fractured, my smokes flattened, and the canopy in shreds, wrapped round the prop of a Mustang. Another couple of turns and I'd have been in there too. All I got was a busted finger, a bang on the nose, and a rollicking from Val when she read it in the papers next day.'

Mervyn Green - again a man of strong opinion

Above: The close link between Falcons and the highest level of sport parachuting was demonstrated in 1968 when Britain won bronze in team accuracy: three of the four were current Falcons – Fourth man was 'Red Devil' Brian David. (Photo courtesy of Doug Peacock)

They jumped from just below the 3,000 foot cloud base, and all landed safe but fast in the target area. Geoff, however, was dragged by his billowing 'chute off the grass and across the concrete, straight towards the turning propellor of a Mustang fighter whose pilot, against regulations, was warming his engine. Geoff didn't see it ...

' ... Before I could get the canopy down I was

who knew what was best for his Team - had fewer problems during his year as Leader in 1969, although he was a little unlucky at the Paris Airshow that year. The Team performed well, not only to the applause of the French crowd but also before the BBC cameras. Raymond Baxter concluded his commentary to British viewers by saying, 'The winds are extremely high but the Falcons have just

Top left: Falcons in Hong Kong in 1971.
Standing L to R: Myself, Gwynne Morgan,
Harry Parkinson, Doug Dewar, Doug Peacock,
Sid Garrard, Alan Jones. Kneeling L to R:
Henry MacDonald, Snowy Robertson, Bob Souter.
Missing injured at this stage were Ray Willis,
David Ross, and Alan Rhind.

Left: Landing in the urban jungle, still smoking.

Right: Tracking across Hong Kong harbour.
(page 74)

completed a breathtaking display in the most difficult conditions.'

Merv was understandably peeved when on his return to PTS he received no plaudits for the 'breathtaking display' but was reprimanded for having dropped the Team in 'extremely high winds'.

The basic skills of body flight and precision landing being demonstrated by the Falcons were similar to although not as precise as those of the sport parachutist involved in style and accuracy competition. Although the 1961 authorisation of the Team had allowed for its members to participate in competition as well as display, a conscious decision had subsequently been made at PTS to concentrate on the primary role of display. Those who also wished to compete were encouraged to do so through the Royal Air Force Sport Parachuting Association (RAFSPA) formed in 1963. Amongst those Falcons who competed at the highest level were Geordie Charlton and Brian Clark-Sutton who were in the British Team for the 1966 World Championships. Brian also represented Britain at the 1967 Adriatic Cup Meet in Yugoslavia. During team training for the event, he suffered a particularly severe opening shock. He took his stiff neck to a doctor who diagnosed torn muscles. Brian continued to practice, then began the competition. He jumped well, but in constant pain. Shortly before the final sequence of jumps, he sought another doctor, who called for X-rays.

'Your neck is broken,' he told Brian. 'Any of

Left: PC over Hong Kong. 'In retrospect,' said Doug Peacock, 'I suppose the risks were there ...' (page 75)

those subsequent jumps could have killed you.'

Sadly, that injury ended the parachuting career of one of Britain's most promising young jumpers of the time.

At the 1968 World Championships, Britain gained third place and bronze medals in the 4-man accuracy event - the best ever by a British men's team, and not yet surpassed. Three of those four were Falcons - Geordie Charlton, Ken Mapplebeck, and Doug Peacock.

Not everyone enjoyed that level of skill - particularly not the officers who led the Team. Their career brought them early and relatively inexperienced to spend one year as deputy, and another as leader. They relied heavily upon the guidance of their knowledgeable NCOs, particularly the Team Flight Sergeants. These worthy characters were not averse to a smile at their expense, as David Cobb recalls...

'My first full display was at Jurby, Isle Of Man, in April 1969. It was a cold windy day and I was in the second group to leave the Argosy and track downwind to the opening point. Merv Green, the Leader, left with the first group, and Flight Sergeant Terry Allen was left to measure the gap for the second group which included Sergeant Les Alworthy and myself on our first display. Now Terry had a sense of humour ... After what seemed several minutes but in fact was only about ten seconds he despatched the second group but held Les and myself for several seconds more before giving a follow-me sign and leaving the aircraft. In free fall I was astonished to find that I was over the sea, and that some distance to the south was the Isle Of Man. Terry was now a dot in the distance as he tracked towards it, Les trying hard to follow. Terry had always realised that tracking was not my strong point, and had decided that I needed a little encouragement. I set off in a buffeting track, but as my trigonometry was better than my tracking I realised that my only chance of making the DZ was to pull high and let the wind carry me in, so I pulled at 3,500 instead of the usual 2,000 feet and arrived on the target only a minute and a half after the others...'

David vowed during that long and lonely descent under the canopy that when he became leader he would devise a new free fall pattern that wouldn't require so much tracking - at least, not from him.

The display that he subsequently devised with Doug Peacock as his Team Flight Sergeant was a much refined adaption of the 1961 bomb-burst. The first men out would form a four-man star - by then a standard accomplishment - while the rest of the Team would track outwards from it to provide the initial bomb-burst effect, then turn and fly back to the foursome who would create another and smaller bomb burst as they split and dived outwards to their individual opening points. Variations on this theme have been displayed by Falcons to this day.

This new display pattern for 1970 was practiced at RAF Sharjah in the Gulf, a new venue for winter training. The team also had to familiarise itself with a new aircraft, for the Argosy was now replaced by the C130 Hercules. And David Cobb had to practice his spotting ...

'The first few descents at Sharjah were fraught with spotting problems. I successfully spread the team all over the desert. "Sir," said one, "Could we have something on desert survival techniques in your next briefing?"

David wanted to take the aircraft off and practice his spotting alone with Doug Peacock, without the embarrassment of misplacing most of his Team. But Doug persuaded him to take the Team and get more practice runs by dropping them one at a time. After all, they were fit young men quite capable of trudging a fair distance through soft sand with a 'chute bundled on their back. They might even see the funny side of it.

Doug Peacock was the first of the Flight Sergeants to be given the title of Team Coach. He, Terry Allen before him, and those who followed have provided the experienced judgement, the cool expertise, and the example of disciplined conduct upon which the Falcons have been built. Above all they have been at the shoulder of their Team Leaders with gentle suggestion whenever it has been called for. And

Below: Team Leader Johnny Johnston introduces the 1974 Team to King Hussein of Jordan after a display in Amman. Shown here L to R are John Mace, Peter Watson, Andy Sweeney and Joe France. John is grimacing because a mal-functioned 'chute had thrown one leg into the rigging lines and he has spent most of his descent hanging upside down.

occasionally when it hasn't.

1971 was a truly international year for the Falcons. With Alan Jones as Leader, they began the season by going round the world, via Australia. Their fame did not precede them. The manifest of crew and passengers signalled ahead to Darwin included 'sixteen Falcons'. The aircraft was met by practically the entire resources of the Northern Territory vetinary service. The Team was better known by the time it left Australia. After a month of pre-season training at the Australian Parachute Training School at Williamtown, they toured the country for another month, giving displays at Perth, Adelaide, Brisbane, Canberra, Sydney and Townsville.

That summer season included displays in Sweden, Germany, Italy, and France. Then came Hong Kong … Doug Peacock, Team Coach for what was undoubtedly the greatest challenge presented to the Falcons until that time - and

rarely exceeded since, given the nature of equipment then in use - remembers it well ...

'We were scheduled to jump at various venues in the City as well as up-country in the New Territories. The centrepiece of these demos was the Government Stadium, set in a natural bowl with cliffs on three sides and a six-lane highway on the fourth. Six times we were to jump there. At night. Jump-ships would be three helicopters at 3,000 feet, at which height wind speeds at night would be in the order of 20 knots. We were also warned that anabatic and katabatic turbulence within the bowl was likely to be pronounced. We nodded wisely, then went away to find out what it meant. Winds flowing up or down the contours, we discovered.

'In consequence it was a distinctly thoughtful bunch who visited the stadium to recce the place from the ground. Heights of obstacles were computed, approach lines considered, overshoots and undershoots mentally discarded: there weren't any. We also checked it out from the air. From 3,000 feet, as always, things looked distinctly better. In retrospect, I suppose, the risks were there. The PC and a front-mounted non-steerable reserve were hardly the kit for a jump into a small arena in the middle of a densely built area, close to the sea, in 20-knot winds, at night. However, that was the job and none of us doubted that we could do it ...

'We waddled out to the "choppers" at Kai Tak about nine o'clock for the first demo, festooned with 'chutes, life-jackets, smoke brackets, torches to illuminate the canopies when they were open, lights to illuminate the altimeters - all the paraphernalia pertaining to a night demo close to deep water. As the aircraft flew over the harbour towards Hong Kong the view from the open door was dramatically spectacular; the

Below: Falcons Ray Willis, Bob Souter, Ty Barraclough, and Joe France - seen here training over Cyprus - were twice British 4–way Relative Work champions during the 1970s.

whole waterfront of Wan Chai was a blaze of lights with be-jewelled towers jutting up from the illuminated ribbons that were the main highways, while the mountainside of the 1600-foot Peak loomed in the background, totally black.

'From the lead "chopper" I could see at least six illuminated stadiums. Which was mine? I hoped the pilot knew ... Then I recognized it as he made straight for it.

'I started my stopwatch as I left the aircraft over the mountainside about 800 yards past the stadium and pulled on exactly eleven seconds. As the canopy came out I saw the shape of Snowy going past me, still in free fall. Wrong. He should have been at my level. He opened below me and started running hard for the stadium, with the sodium flare in the centre and its smoke blowing towards us. Wrong again, especially as I was by then right above it at 1,000 feet facing into the upper wind and being blown back towards the harbour. Worrying moments, but all at once, as we came below the level of the main hill-line, the 20-knot uppers decreased to zero and we were left with a gentle approach to the bowl and we could take those Para-Commanders just where we wanted. As we came into the radius of the stadium lighting we pulled the smokes and slid comfortably one after the other into the centre circle of the soccer pitch in a series of light, running stand-ups. Judging by the din, 30,000 highly vocal orientals thought it was magic. We were a bit impressed ourselves.'

Between the night-jumps into the stadium there were high altitude shows during the day into some equally spectacular arenas: Aberdeen fishing port, Kai Tak airfield, a soccer stadium at

Yueng Long close to the border with Red China, Victoria Park on the waterfront in 18-knot surface winds ... 'A real rock'n roll in between the skyscrapers, everybody piling in backwards onto the dusty soccer pitch with feet and knees tight together, no fancy running stand-ups this time ...' Doug Peacock recalls. By contrast, the racecourse (the old one, on Hong Kong Island) seemed indecently extensive. Henry McDonald, however, overdid his outbound 'track' and couldn't get back to the opening point above a well-populated ridge. As the rest of the Team headed for the race-goers, Henry turned his back on them and went visiting on his own - to the Government Stadium again, on the other side of the ridge. It was deserted. He landed (dead centre, he said, as jumpers always do when no one is watching them), bundled his chute, climbed over the gate, thumbed a lift back to the racecourse, and was in the Members' Bar supping a cool beer almost as soon as the rest of us.

The nature and the intensity of jumping, the hard surfaces, and the unkind surrounds for the few who missed the DZs took their toll in minor injuries, but Hong Kong was an outstanding success, and a milestone in Falcons history. Wisely perhaps, the potential for urban jumping was not pursued until the next generation of parachutes greatly reduced the risks that were undoubtedly - but most exhilaratingly - taken in Hong Kong in 1971.

Tragedy tracked the Falcons through the later stages of the 1971 season and into 1972. Ex-Falcon Sergeant Ralph Lee died with the rest of the crew when a Hercules in which he was flying as despatcher for an airborne exercise in Italy crashed into the sea off Pisa. A month later Flying

Above: BBC's 'Blue Peter' presenter John Noakes completed a military free fall course at PTS, culminating in a jump from 25,000 feet, filmed by Bob Souter who is seen here escorting him during an earlier training jump.

Officer Ralph Ramshaw also died in the sea. After some basic free fall training at Abingdon he had attended a course with the US Army at Fort Bragg where as the best novice free faller he had won a trophy almost as tall as himself. Whilst training as a potential Falcon leader in Cyprus, on a drop over Ladies Mile DZ which is extensive but sea-bordered, he opened his canopy high and was drifted inexorably towards the waves. He splashed down only 100 yards from the shore, but in carrying out his emergency drills as briefed, became entangled in rigging lines, and drowned.

A few months later during pre-season training for 1972 the whole Team came close to death. The fair weather for that year's detachment had been found in northern Italy, on an air strip at Ampugnano, near Pisa. The training was good. At the end of it, the Team gave a display for the local population and dignitaries. Speeches and presentations were made, farewells said, and the Team climbed into their Andover for the return flight to Pisa, and home. Half way down the runway the aircraft slewed, tipped, cartwheeled, crashed back onto its belly and burst into flames. It was a wonder that any got out. Four didn't: two members of the crew died, as did Sergeant Roy Bullen of the Team, and Squadron Leader Bill Last who was my deputy CO at PTS.

Shortly after the funerals in England, the Falcons held their annual press-day as planned. One of the reporters on the Andover noted that the jumpers were favouring the seats towards the rear of the fuselage. He asked if there was any reason. 'Sure. It doesn't burn so well back here,' came the reply, and with it the all-important grin.

That wry humour of the parachutist, and the phlegmatic leadership of Gwynne Morgan saw the 1972 Falcons through the season as though tragedy had never been.

The humour was well employed and the phlegmatic nature well tested when Gwynne made his last jump of the season. It was at Teeside. Gwynne spotted the run, called for the green, and dived from the door. To his dismay he found himself alone in the sky. Nobody had followed him. By pre-arrangement with the show organisers and the aircrew, the Team had planned that the boss's final descent as Leader would be a lonely and memorable one. They followed him on the next pass.

His successor as Leader was Alec Jackson. When Alec had volunteered for PJI training, his wife Sue had expressed concern. Wasn't parachuting terribly dangerous? Not at all, Alec had assured her, and had duly qualified. His first job had been in support of an airborne exercise in Italy when the Hercules with Ralph Lee on board had crashed. Then his close friend Ralph Ramshaw had died, putting Alec with all of three free fall descents into contention for training as a Falcon leader. During that training Alec had been one of those who somehow scrambled from the flaming Andover at Ampugnano, pictured widely in the British papers...

'Thus,' said Alec, 'after 55 free fall descents, 6 military funerals, a photograph on the front page of the *News Of The World*, and a wife who no longer believed a word I said about parachuting, I commenced my Falcons career, barely 12 months after joining No. 1 PTS.'

Alec survived his year as deputy to have a particularly good season as Leader, with 48 displays completed out of the 56 programmed, almost one third of them overseas. He remembers in particular the pre-season training in Jordan, where Amman now provided the clear skies, but where it was still advisable to get the jumps in early, before the heat and the turbulence of the day began to play tricks on parachutists ...

'Picture a perfect Arabian dawn, an empty Jordanian desert and a solitary goat-herd fast asleep with his flock and nothing but camel-thorn and the Israelis between himself and the Mediterranean 500 miles away. Suddenly with hardly a footfall or a heavy breath a dozen Falcons land all around him - his eyes roll, his goats flee, and our intrepid interpreter Mal Reed wishes him good morning, what wonderful goats, and isn't Allah bountiful ...'

On his final display the Team treated a wary Alec with less subtlety than they had employed on Gwynne Morgan. Preparing for the drop onto Akrotiri in Cyprus, he was leapt upon by former Combined Services heavyweight boxer Joe France and two RAF back-row forwards who trussed him like a chicken and waved goodbye as they stepped from the doors.

He was allowed another descent to pass the leader's baton in free fall to his successor Johnny Johnston.

The 1974 season was curtailed by the fuel crisis caused by the 'six-day-war' in the Middle East, but it had its share of highlights. There was the

Above: Every Falcon trains first as a PJI, and that training begins with a full military course as undertaken by the men he will eventually train - the airborne soldier. When Brian Stevenson, later to become a Falcon leader, commenced his parachuting career in 1977 he was in illustrious company. Prince Charles, as Colonel-In-Chief of the Parachute Regiment qualified for his airborne wings on the same basic military course.

show at RAF Gatow when the wind conditions required the Team to open their 'chutes above East Berlin and drift over the 'wall' to land on the airfield in West Berlin. There was the Paris Airshow, where the target crosses had to be laid on grass charred by the jet-blast of the Russian 'Concordski', which had its parking space next to the DZ. And if anyone wished it elsewhere,

they deeply regretted their words when before their eyes on the second day Concordski crashed in flames.

They may have had less shows, but the 1974 Team didn't lack publicity. They led fifty-nine PJIs and Army free fall trainees over the sill of a Hercules for the largest free fall drop then achieved in Britain, and made a film called 'They Own The Sky' which took the Falcons into the homes of the nation through BBC and ITV. The aerial camera-work was done by Sergeant Doug Fletcher using a new GSAP Gun Camera.

The tail-end of the fuel crisis also curtailed the 1975 season. Andovers and helicopters sometimes replaced the greedier Hercules, and any events that smacked of frivolity were cancelled by the Ministry Of Defence. To the annoyance of the Team one of those was the drop onto Morecambe beach to open the Miss World Competition. Peter Watson as Team Leader was especially upset: he had been invited to judge. But there were four fine displays at different locations in Denmark to commemorate the 25th anniversary of the Royal Danish Air Force, and a drop at Rygge in Norway in awesome upper winds and 20 mph on the surface. So accurate was that drop despite the conditions that when Ty Barraclough lowered the Norwegian flag on its suspension cord and Terry Cooke followed with the Union Jack they were so close above the Royal stand that it was feared they had garroted the King of Norway.

The insistence throughout Falcons history of this accuracy on the DZ above all else - even at the expense of elaborate free fall display - was fully although tragically justified at the Paris Airshow that year ...

'The French Army Display Team jumped

immediately before us, while we were airborne for our own drop,' says Peter Watson. 'They concentrated on going for a large "link" rather than a controlled canopy display. Predictably, they landed all over the place. What's more, one of their number had a malfunction and sadly went in. I had heard all this over my headphones and knew that we had to pull off an outstanding display to redeem the image of display jumping. I called for a special effort, but did not explain why, fearing that news of the fatality would not have done much for morale. I needn't have worried. The Team were superb, and the display was immaculate. Needless to say, they had all known of the incident and were far more concerned at my solemnity. "We were worried you might not disconnect your lead, Boss!" they said, for I did have this habit at particularly difficult displays of forgetting to unplug my headset before jumping …'

1975 had its lighter moments, as all Falcon seasons do. As at Saddleworth, Oldham, where on a small DZ in difficult conditions Sergeant Steve Rowe put his boot through the Town Band's big base drum, and at the reception afterwards a ravenous Graham Pierce inadvertently ate the first prize in the fancy-cake competition.

Although the Ministry Of Defence cut back on overseas displays in 1976, the Falcons gave more demonstrations than ever before - sixty-four out of a planned seventy-four. Winter training for the first time took place in El Centro, Texas - to become until this day the major venue for the out-of-season detachments, not only for Falcons but for basic free fall

Right: Falcon faces, looking for that drop zone from the door of the Hercules. Phil Kelly, Bob Kent, Joe McCready, Simon Bales.

Above: No Falcon likes the low show. Forced down to 2,200 feet by cloud, it's out the door and pull – like Joe McCready here. (Photo by Tony Betteridge)

trainees and test jumpers from Boscombe Down.

But in spite of the good season and the excellent training detachments, the Teams of 1976 and 1977 felt keenly the frustration that had been creeping up on Falcons over the previous few years...

By 76 the PC was positively old fashioned. It had given good service, and its inception ten years earlier had added greatly to accuracy and safety. But although it had countered the wind to a previously unknown extent it had not fully outwitted the old enemy. Accurate assessment of release and opening points, good spotting, sometimes a sacrifice of free fall patterns, and skilled canopy work by team and individual were still essential to bring the Falcons to their target. It didn't always happen. Geoff Diggle jumping during the 70s as a sergeant and later to lead the

Team himself recalls some of the problems ...

'Colchester Tattoo was always a particularly exciting challenge and I remember one demo with a maximum long release point and the wind on limits. Clive Hillman put us out on a stack pull exactly on the release point which was a roundabout somewhere in the middle of town 1400 yards away from the Tattoo DZ. Fortunately the wind was straight down the line and we were slap in the middle of the wind cone. One of the lads was high and sailed over the VIP box on the edge of the arena heading straight for the thick trees that seemed to have no break in them, but he found a gap and landed safely. The bowling green adjacent to the arena at Colchester was always a favourite escape landing ground and the elderly bowlers soon became unperturbed by our unannounced arrivals on matinee days.'

Geoff was a relative lightweight, usually the last man in the 'stack' and prone to suffer from what he called the 'dandelion syndrome' - the inability to land anywhere when caught in the rising air of thermals. At Finningley on a particularly hot day he was under the canopy for at least seven minutes, and despite all his efforts he landed two miles away from the DZ.

The frustrations of the Falcons in the mid-1970s rose from the knowledge that a parachute now existed that would have relieved them of the occasional indignities of landing off target, or being 'thermalized'. They felt too that they were being left behind - literally - by other display teams better equipped than themselves: teams equipped with the new generation of parachute now flying through the skies. Yes - flying. For the era of the 'square' ram-air parachute was well under way.

CHAPTER FIVE

FALCONS GO SQUARE

At the time that the Para-Commander was first appearing on the international parachuting scene in 1964, American Dominic Jalbert filed a patent for the canopy that would eventually replace it. It was a canopy that would revolutionize parachuting: the ram-air square parachute.

In fact, it isn't square: it's rectangular. It comprises two sheets of ripstop nylon connected by airfoil shaped ribs to make a layer of open-ended cells into which air is 'rammed' during flight, then compressed to inflate the canopy and expelled to impart forward drive. It is an inflated fabric wing, with inbuilt forward speed of up to 25 mph. Speed and direction are controllable, to provide the parachutist - once experienced in its use - with a power-packed precision instrument.

Another advantage offered by the square was that it came in a 'piggyback' assembly, in which the reserve was carried above the main canopy in the back-pack, thus completely clearing the front of the body for free fall, to make flight skills more effective - particularly tracking. Some round canopies had been stowed in 'piggyback' systems, but not the PCs of the Falcons.

PJIs began jumping squares in the early '70s, but as sport parachutists, not as Falcons. In 1972 RAFSPA formed its own small display team operating out of Abingdon with the Association's civilian registered DH Rapide, to give demonstrations at functions and fetes throughout southern England. The 'Robins'

The square parachute brought the Falcons into smaller drop zones with greater precision than ever before. (Photo by Tony Betteridge)

Above: Although the loose canopy stack is prefered for major Falcon displays, Canopy Relative Work is practiced and occasionally demonstrated. Here, a 'quadraplane' formation is breaking up for landing.

they were called. 'Picking up the crumbs left by the Falcons,' some added. Mostly the team members were ex-Falcons. In 1972 the Robins acquired three long-line Paraplanes from Peter Schofield, at that time leading the very effective Red Devils team. They and the Robins, being self-supporting rather than military-funded teams, were free of the constraints of Service procurement systems. The squares greatly enhanced the performances by the Robins, but early versions were prone to deployment problems, and to instability in turbulent winds. Canopy malfunctions added to the excitement of the occasional Robins display, and instability close to the ground during a drop into a north-London football field fractured both of Flying Officer Peter Smout's legs - which wouldn't prevent him returning to lead the Falcons in 1979.

By the mid 1970s the design problems had been largely resolved, and all self-respecting sport and display parachutists had gone square: except the Falcons, tied to a procurement system that didn't share their impatience.

At last, in 1976, authority was granted for the Team to be equipped with the American 'Strato Cloud' parachute. They didn't come in time for the 1977 display season, but were available for that winter's training in El Centro.

The Falcons had at last gone 'square'.

The transition of the Team from round to square was fortunately in the hands of Flight Sergeant Joe France, Team Coach. Joe had already served three years with the Team as a sergeant, and was one of the foremost sport parachutists of the day, specialising in sequential relative work. He, Bob Souter, Ray Willis and Ty Barraclough - all Falcons - had twice won the National 4-man RW championship, and twice represented Britain in World Championships.

Although a 'relative' competitor rather than an accuracy jumper, Joe was an experienced user of the square, with the ability to pass on that experience in a quiet but if necessary forceful manner. Sensibly, Joe and his Team Leader for 1978 - Roger Nicolle - resisted the temptation of excessive change to the display format. They accepted gratefully the greater potential of the square to get them safely to their targets, and gloried in the modern appearance of their new 'chutes in their distinctive red-white-and-blue pattern as they flew them into the 1978 showgrounds.

The concept of a canopy 'stack' with parachutes stepped up above and behind each other had already been adopted for the PCs, partly for visual effect but more importantly to allow for staggered opening heights and to give each parachutist a clear and safe run at his target. Refinements to this system were now possible, but other than putting himself in the position of low man to lead in the others, Joe wisely kept the emphasis during this first square season on individual canopy handling rather than team skills. Those would come the following year.

'Square will get you there' became the cry of the 1978 Team. But it would only get you there if you knew where you were going, as Joe France recalls...

'Jumping into Guernsey from 12,000 feet in front of Roger Nicolle's home town, I had my head out of the port door - the boss spotting

Right: Team Leader Geoff Diggle tries to 'spot' the release point through cloud in 1981. (page 93)

FALCONS

Above: During the 1980s, Falcons appeared above some notable landmarks throughout Britain. For example, Blackpool Pier...

Top right: ... the Tower Of London...

Bottom right: ... Liverpool's Liver Building.

from the starboard side. I had the ground flare and drop zone visual, and eyeballed it until overhead when I climbed out into the air deflector to prepare for the six-way from the door. After exit I would immediately check the release point and the ground flare again, and once in the link I would call the break dependent upon how good the spot had been. This time when I looked for the ground flare I could see several thousand of them - or rather I could see several thousand greenhouse window panes reflecting the sun. On opening I had no idea which was the real flare, nor where the DZ was. I stooged around pretending I knew where I was going, the rest of the guys following me like lambs. After approximately one minute I had about given up any hope when I located the DZ, and was just able to take them in. Nobody knew until later how fortunate the team was that day to hit the target.'

The following year Joe, with Peter Smout as Team Leader, introduced the close canopy stack. The square had brought a new dimension to sport parachuting. Unlike the round canopy which would collapse if its air was stolen by another parachute flying below it, the square with its reliance on horizontal air flow could be manoeuvred into vertical formations, with parachutists actually standing on each other's shoulders. Canopy Relative Work (CRW) was the name given to this physical linking of parachutes. Those of us brought up to keep well away from other parachutists viewed with admiration but some alarm these attempts at purposeful proximity.

Exciting and impressive though it was, and although Team members practiced contact

Top left, bottom left and above: Horse Guards Parade provided one of the most challenging drop zones to the teams of 1979 and 1983. 'The ground is close enough when jumping from 2,500 feet, but London looked even closer that day ...' (page 95)

CRW, it was not introduced into Falcons display. To have done so would have required opening heights that would have detracted from both free fall display and accurate team landings, and the level of skill required would have dominated training at the expense of other aspects. Nor could smoke canisters be carried on the ankles for CRW. Not as technically skillful but still visually impressive was the no-contact canopy stack devised by Joe with Peter Smout. This built on previous experience of loosely stacking

the PCs on opening and for approach to the target. Now, using the better flying characteristics of the square, the stack was refined. Each man had his allocated slot in the formation, and would take his position above and behind the Team Coach in the final seconds of the free fall phase. All would operate their 'chutes on his signal so that they opened already in a semblance of the stack. Adjustments would then be made under the canopies to create the tiered formation, all following the lower man towards the ground, all streaming smoke. And at twenty miles per hour, the smoke streamed most effectively.

Variations of the 1979 canopy stack have featured since then as another aspect of Falcons

display: formation flight under the canopy.

The transition from round to square could be dangerous, particularly for those with well established 'round' reflexes. Like me. Serving reluctantly in a non-para post as OC Administrative Wing at RAF St Mawgan, I jumped as a guest with the Falcons at the Station's International Air Day in 1979. Peter Smout politely asked if I would pull a little high, so as not to get involved in the jockeying for positions in the stack. 'Would you mind keeping out the bloody way' is what he really wanted to say. I didn't mind at all. After a panoramic fall from 12,000 feet I had a more leisurely view from under the canopy at 3,000 of the Cornish cliffs and beaches stretching south to Newquay

and north to Trevose Head. Nice. Then, with the Team's 'chutes closely clustered about the target below me, I approached in solitary state, attracting the full attention of crowd and commentator. How fitting it would have been for the 'father of the Falcons' as they were calling me just then to have stepped nonchalantly out of the sky for an easy stand-up landing right on the target. Instead of which, at some 100 feet my ingrained PC instinct took over in the form of a hard pull on one toggle, designed to hook me onto the cross. The grass and the target and the upturned faces tilted and blurred and I crashed in sideways in a cloud of dust and an explosion of breath.

'Bloody hell, boss!' murmured a white-faced

Left: International sporting arenas have provided spectacular settings for Falcon displays, such as Brands Hatch ...

Above: ... Cardiff Arms Park ...
Right: ... and Old Trafford.

Peter Smout as I staggered into the line-up. Had I been able to talk, I could have told him that there had been a time when we always landed like that ...

In proper hands the square was not only an impressive flying machine. By offering a far more extensive opening 'area', it reduced the number of occasions when free fall display patterns had to be sacrificed in favour of reaching a tight opening point. Also, it allowed Team leaders and coaches to jump in those borderline cases that would not have been

The annual change of leadership of the Falcons is marked by passing the ceremonial baton. Here, Steve Darling hands it to Dave Paveley at the close of the 1994 season - thirty five years after the first all-British baton pass, achieved by 'Falcon Fathers' John Thirtle and Peter Hearn with a rolled-up sick-bag from the Beverley.

acceptable under round canopies: gave more latitude to that instinctive reaction by spirited yet responsible leadership that in difficult circumstances says 'Yes ... we can do it ... let's go...!'

Geoff Diggle, who returned as a Flight Lieutenant to lead the Team in 1981, remembers such an occasion when he 'did it' at RAF Church Fenton...

'A real claggy day, but a full date with the Press and TV who were to spend all day with us filming our preparation, interviewing team members, filming the display from the air and the ground - the full works. P-hour approached, with the aircraft full of TV and papparazi, and total cloud cover over the DZ. As usual I had studied the aerial photo and the Ordnance Survey map, and the identifying markers around the release point were very prominent - if only I could see them! I made a dummy run. No sign of the ground. A second pass for a live run, then a third, still couldn't see anything. Last pass, running out of time and looking bad. Went overhead the airfield, and still nothing. Suddenly, off to port, a hole appeared in the cloud showing a particular-shaped copse of trees I had identified as being exactly adjacent to the release point. I knew exactly where I was. No time for red on or green on. I just said over the intercom "We're off," gave the thumb and left the aircraft. The display was a great success...'

It surely would have been, with twelve canopies ghosting out of the cloud, and not a sign of the aeroplane that had discharged them. Geoff wouldn't have tried it had they not had squares on their backs.

Since the early 1970s the number of Falcon

**Above: 'We sat down to argue over the map again ...'
Dave Griffiths and Ali McDonald try to find their quarry.
(page 102)**

displays had been creeping up. One hundred were planned for 1980, seventy-eight of them completed. Significantly, the nature of the venues was changing too. At one time, major air shows had provided almost the only stage for the Falcons. Although air displays still featured prominently in the Team's annual programme, an increasing proportion of appearances were now at 'civil' or sporting functions not necessarily connected with aviation or the Armed Forces. Authority was begining to appreciate the publicity and recruiting value of the Falcons outside the air-show circuit - where in any case they were often displaying to the already-converted. This presentation of the Team to a wider audience was boosted by the introduction of the square parachute, which made 'arena jumping' a more feasible alternative to the traditional 'crowd-line' shows on the airfields. We had introduced urban jumping in Hong Kong in 1971, but that had been before its time: before the square canopy reduced the risks

to a level that was acceptable for every-day display. So throughout the 1980s the drop zones became increasingly intimate.

Seaside resorts in particular began to feature more prominently in the programme: Blackpool, Eastbourne, Torbay, Lyme Regis, Cromer, Whitby, Teignmouth, Rhyl, Weymouth, Mevagissey, Plymouth, and Sherringham.

The Falcons also jumped at major sporting events: at Brands Hatch, Donnington Park, Doncaster racecourse, the Portuguese Grand Prix, and most spectacularly into San Diego's Jack Murphy football stadium each time the Team trained at El Centro in the autumn. Their greatest disappointment would come in 1991 when low cloud over Twickenham prevented the planned drop into the stadium, carrying the match ball, to open the first Rugby Union World Cup. A subsequent drop into Cardiff Arms Park in 1992 was some consolation. Old Trafford - for a Test Match - has recently being added to the list of sporting venues.

And there were the pure 'urban' drop zones, like the lawn outside Liverpool's Liver Building, the Tower of London, and Horse Guards' Parade, first in 1979 then again in 1983. Someone watching from the ground on that second display remarked how easy the Falcons had made it look. It wasn't easy ...

'It was difficult because we were limited by London Air Traffic Control to 2,500 feet, and because they also dictated the run-in track,' says Brian Stevenson, leader for 1983. 'In other words we had a cross-wind run-in, which has to be even more accurately followed than usual in order to achieve the correct air point for opening. I knew that if we missed our opening point we would miss the DZ, the Prime

Minister, the Chief of Defence Staff and the 5,000 other spectators, and that there was no alternative landing site other than the Thames. On top of that every national newspaper and TV Company flew with us in the Hercules, so I knew that my every action would be recorded. Pressure ? Not really .....!

'It was a murky day with poor visibility, and spotting was not easy. I knew from the plotted run-in track that we were due to open over Charing Cross Station, but as we ran in over the mass that is the centre of London I could not recognise anything. I remember seeing Lords Cricket Ground but in my mind I could not orientate its position relative to Horse Guards' Parade. I asked the pilot over the intercom if he could see the Thames, but he replied that the

Below: Janet Ellis, BBC's 'Blue Peter' presenter, training in the suspended harness for the series of free fall descents that she made with the Falcons in 1984 and 1985.

visibility was so poor that he could see very little. What chance have I got then, I remember thinking!

'Eventually I spotted Trafalgar Square coming up and knew that the River could only be seconds away. We were off course but I could not call a dummy run because Air Traffic insisted that we only had one attempt to achieve the drop, so I calmly said to the pilot "45 degrees right". He didn't say a word, but immediately the Hercules banked severely starboard, playing havoc with the Team and the assembled TV and Press, but I didn't notice. I was transfixed, staring in the direction of the air point I knew we had to achieve, and willing the aircraft to make it before we overflew the River. We didn't quite get there, but we were close enough so I raised my thumb and out we went.

'The ground is close enough when jumping from 2,500 feet, but London looked even closer

that day and I remember thinking as I left the Hercules that this was not the place to have a malfunction. Well, nobody did, and we all landed safely, feeling tremendously exhilarated and extremely satisfied.'

Brian also had a few problems at Ilfracombe, parachuting onto the pier ...

'With the benefit of hindsight I would not attempt this parachute display again. The pier was flanked by 300-foot cliffs on one side, the open sea and the harbour packed with moored yachts on the other. To make matters worse on the day, a Wessex helicopter and a double-

correctly and we began to form the stack. The first hint of trouble was when canopies started to collapse due to air turbulence and team members fell up to 250 feet before re-inflation. At the same time the Team Coach, Flight Sergeant Ali Macdonald, could not control his parachute at all and had to abandon the display, finally landing on the headland beyond the harbour. The Team was now without its "lead-in" man and as the turbulence increased it became a survival exercise and eleven individual approaches to the pier. Thankfully we all made it safely, but as we lined up to take the salute I

Above: Squadron Leader Gordon Hannam of the Red Arrows tries flying without an aeroplane during an exchange of 'experiences' between Arrows and Falcons in 1986. (page 107)

decker bus were parked on the pier itself, in addition to the crowds of spectators. The weather was fine but windy, and we did not expect to jump as the wind was forecast to be out of limits. However, when we arrived overhead the DZ advised us that the wind was only ten knots, but what we did not know was that the wind at 300 feet had risen in excess of thirty since the DZ party had taken their last reading. Nevertheless, as we exited at 12,000 feet with a release point of 3,000 yards, I had an uneasy feeling. All twelve parachutes opened

vowed never to parachute onto the end of a pier again ...'

Falcon leaders, chosen for their spirit and initiative as well as their potential free fall ability, naturally seek to make and leave their mark upon the Team. Primarily they do so by maintaining the long-established standards of excellence, and some have done so by introducing new display patterns. So, in 1984, Dave Griffiths changed the aerial bomb-burst to the 'arrowhead' formation, and in 1985 Mike Milburn changed it

Above: 'Tandem Jumping' provides another form of accelerated introduction to the sensations of free fall. Falcon Nigel Rogoff is the tandem master, his pupil a member of the RAF Central Band. (Photo Alistair Wright)

back again ... But despite variations in pattern the concept has remained the same as that determined at the very foundation of the RAF Parachute Display Team - the demonstration of movement in free fall before placing the whole team in close but safe proximity at a pre-determined opening point, from which they can exhibit accurate landings as a group. To this, as we have seen, the square parachute had added the potential for canopy formation flying.

There were those who, during the initial enthusiasm for CRW, still thought that this should feature in Falcons display. The Red Devils were doing it. And the Royal Marines Team had specialised in it to such an extent that they were the world's best 'canopy stackers'. But CRW of that standard could only be achieved at the expense of other aspects of parachute display, both in training and in performance. Above all, mass accuracy around the target remained the primary aim of Falcons display. The 'arena' jumps for the broader audiences that the Team was now reaching had emphasised even more the PR value of accurate landings, not only because they were impressive, but also because they took place so close to the crowd. This immediate availability of performers to their audience - shaking hands, signing autographs, nonchalant chat, handing out Team brochures, answering those questions - is a bonus offered by few aerial performers. It is much envied by aerobatic teams whose audiences are so often no more than a tilted blur of admiring but impersonal faces. To be able to see the parachutist, to be able to touch him, to be able to smell the acrid smoke still clinging to him from his ankle canisters - that has long been one of the great appeals of show jumping to its earthbound audience.

So wise heads decided that nothing should detract from the well founded principles of Falcons display, and in particular from those accurate, mass landings. Instead of advanced CRW, they concentrated on improving their no-contact canopy stack. They brought it together more swiftly, formed it more tightly, added more movement to it in the form of wide sweeps and controlled spirals, led by the Team Coach as low man, drawing concerted curves of smoke against the sky, then the whole team turning into wind for the final approach to the target crosses, peppering them with stand-up landings …

This visual effectiveness of the Falcons stack, and Joe France's pioneering and leadership of it, were recognised in dramatic fashion in 1988. Doctor Ewe Beckman was head of the International Parachuting Committee at a time when it was seeking to have sport parachuting included in the Olympic Games. He had seen the Falcons perform on several occasions in Europe

Left: The Team cameraman prepares to follow Falcons in flight. Video film can be recorded or transmitted live to the ground using the Sonic Air-to-Ground Microwave System. Minolta cameras are used for 'stills'.

Above: For instructional purposes the cameraman films team training over El Centro ... while another cameraman films him.

and thought that a similar display performed by a team of international champions from different countries during the opening ceremony would be an ideal way of introducing parachuting to the audience at Seoul and those watching worldwide on television. To coach the 17-man canopy stack and to lead it into the Olympic stadium, Ewe Beckman asked for Joe France ...

'I implemented all the things I had learnt during 1978-80. Although the parachutists in Seoul under my control were experts in their own right, they still found the pattern difficult to perform at the onset. Eventually, however, they performed on the day to a very high standard in front of 100,000 people in the all-seater stadium, and several million television viewers.'

It was Joe's seven thousand and something jump. When you get to that many you're never quite sure of the exact number.

Delighted though Falcons were to have gone square in 1978, the relationships between the Team and the procurement agencies and engineering authorities who provided and approved the Team's equipment remained a trifle strained. In 1983 with its Strato Clouds due for replacement, the Falcons were re-equipped for Service/political reasons and not through their own choice with a British square parachute, the GQ-236. It was never popular. It malfunctioned too often, and was notoriously unstable in turbulent air, as Flight Lieutenant Derek Warby,

Above: Occasionally, the Chinook helicopter provides an alternative jump platform.

jumping as deputy leader in 1985, discovered …

'The problem was brought home to me in '85 when I experienced a canopy collapse in the final stages of a descent. The result of the collapse was that I dropped onto a concrete dispersal from about 30 feet and fractured my left femor, tibia and fibia as well as losing both cruciate ligaments and rupturing the medial ligament in my knee; a full house!'

Then, later in 1985 during a PTS training exercise in Cyprus, Flight Lieutenant David Michael (not a Falcon) died on Ladies Mile drop zone. Although his death could not be attributed directly to malfunction of the GQ-236, loss of confidence in the parachute was now absolute.

The Team Leader said that he would no longer ask the Team to jump it. OC PTS - Wing Commander Roy McCluskey, who from his experiences as a test-jumper knew much about malfunctions - supported him so vigorously that the British parachute was withdrawn from service and replaced with the American 'XL Cloud', purchased direct from its manufacturer, Paraflite Incorporated. To the credit of the GQ Parachute Company, it persevered with improvements to its range of free fall parachutes, and now provides the reliable and efficient GQ-360 used for high altitude military free fall parachuting.

There remained another problem. 'Square will get you there' was fine. But if the main square canopy opened only partially or not at all, the responsibility for 'getting you there' passed to the reserve parachute. And the reserve parachute used by the Falcons throughout the 1980s wasn't square: it was a steerable round 'chute that offered a much reduced potential for a safe and accurate landing. During 1983, Brian Stevenson had to discard a partially opened Strato Cloud and take to his reserve while 1500 yards out to sea at Blackpool. He couldn't reach the target high on the sands under the reserve canopy, but made the beach by five feet.

The higher malfunction-rate of the GQ-236 in 1984 made the need for a steerable reserve even more acute - particularly over those urban DZs. Mark Perry had to cut away onto his reserve over Witney, and was unable to avoid landing on someone's roof. As usually happens to errant parachutists, he was offered a cup of tea. He took to his reserve again over Newton Abbot, and found a cow pasture this time. Ali McDonald had a closer call at the Liverpool Flower Show that same year ...

'I operated my hand-deployed drogue 'chute but it snagged on my right wrist, and as I attempted to clear it, my bag and lines came out in a classic horse-shoe malfunction. I tried to barrel roll away from the problem, hoping the drogue would free itself, but all I saw was the spread of tangled lines above my head. Looking at it was eating up valuable altitude. I decided to cut away my risers in the hope that at least I could get a little clear air above my head into which I could release the reserve. In fact the airflow pulled the lines and the bag away from my body and ripped off my right glove where the drogue had snagged. I again half rolled onto my side and watched my problem disappear. Not content with just pulling my reserve, I turned

again to fall face to earth to allow for a clean deployment. That nearly cost me my life, for spread below me were the roof-tops of a housing estate, very very close. I pulled, and landed aproximately fifteen seconds later in a children's concrete play-area in central Liverpool.'

Those fifteen seconds under the canopy would have been less than two seconds in free fall. Extreme emergency often elicits from the experienced jumper who has long put fear behind him a form of almost detached technical curiosity. Had Ali McDonald been truly terrified, he might have had that reserve flying a lot quicker.

By the 1980s there was less need for parachutists to be subjected to the embarrassment and potential dangers of 'landing off' if forced to take to their reserve, for there existed square reserve canopies to back up the square mains. PTS first asked for them in 1981 and continued to ask for another nine years before they were eventually provided.

The missing of a drop zone cannot always be attributed to equipment failure. Falcons are not immune to human error. 'Barry Charnock's tree' has entered Falcons folklore, not because he is the only one to have landed in a tree-top but because he wasn't quick enough to get out of it before someone took a photograph. At Culzean Castle in Ayrshire he flew too far down-wind of a tiny, tree-bordered arena, and couldn't claw back over the trees against the 25-knot wind.

Human error rarely occurs in the aircraft. With both the Team Leader and the Coach guiding the pilot onto the calculated release point, and probably with a few other pairs of eyes watching the run-in as well, mistakes in 'spotting' are rare. There was one occasion, however …

'It was the end of a long day in July, the aircraft approaching Newton Abbot racecourse,' says Dave Griffiths, Team Leader in 1984. 'It was the fourth display of the day, everyone tired, the cloud low and the wind high. The DZSO gave us a 1500-yard release point which was a long way for a 2,500 foot drop, which was all the height we could get. The spot would have to be a good one. We consulted the aerial map and plotted the release point right over a distinctive quarry. I spotted from the starboard door, Ali McDonald from the port. I kept giving corrections to the right, Ali to the left. Result was a dummy run. We had another go. Same result. Total disagreement for the first time that season, air turning blue, bewildered team looking on. Yet a third time we had the Hercules snaking all over the sky between Newton Abbot racecourse and that quarry, and yet again we couldn't agree. We sat down to argue over the map again. Eureka! We suddenly realised that since the aerial photograph had been taken, a second and identical quarry had been dug 400 yards away from the original. Ali had been aiming for one, me for the other. We agreed on one of them, hit it on the nose on the next run, piled out, everything fine …'

One major advance in Falcons equipment during the 1980s was the provision - from commercial sources and mostly on generous loan - of video cameras for air-to-air filming. The training value of immediate play-back of free fall performance has proved inestimable. Nor does one any longer hear voices protesting 'Of course it wasn't me who bust the link …'

That eye in the sky tells all. Sergeant Pete Reynolds of the Falcons pioneered the free falling video to such good effect that he was asked to join the British Team in training for the 1981 World Parachuting Championships, in which the British men won bronze in the 4-man sequential RW competition. Peter has subsequently left the RAF for a civilian career as one of the World's leading freefall cameramen.

Whilst the advance of Falcons skills has owed much to improved equipment, it has also been a product of better training systems. In the early 1970s basic free fall experience had been incorporated in the training syllabus of the PJI for the first time. Thereafter, all PJIs would be free fallers, not the selected minority, thus taking from free fall the last of the traditional mystique. Also in the early 1970s, free fall parachuting had been included with other challenging activities in a Tri-Service Adventure Training Scheme, designed to encourage the military qualities of initiative and spirit. Through its sport parachuting facility at Weston-on-the-Green, PTS provided a base for this training. Free fall parachuting was becoming almost normal.

More importantly the free fall training of PJIs - and all military free fallers at PTS - had at the same time broken free of the long and costly system of slow progression in drop height and time in the air. Instead, after intensive ground training, the novice would make his first free fall from 12,000 feet. No longer would he have three seconds of fleeting impression: he would have almost a minute in which to discard his tension and most of his fear; to 'feel' the air and to balance on it - albeit precariously. This was

The 1990 team and other PJI free fallers celebrate twenty-five years of 'Falconry' with this 25-man formation over El Centro.

Falcons have dropped into many spectacular international settings. Sydney harbour provided the backdrop in 1988.

Gibraltar ... another fabulous setting for the
Falcon stack.

achieved by the adaption of the 'buddy system' that I had first seen operated by the professionals of 'Paraventures Incorporated' ten years earlier. At PTS the free fall trainees were already qualified static-line parachutists. After intensive ground training, much of it on a suspended free fall simulator, the pupil would make his first 12,000-foot drop without physical assistance, but with an instructor flying alongside him offering a reassuring grin and explicit hand signals if needed, and providing an instant critique of performance as soon as his feet touched the ground. The ultimate safety factor was an automatic opening device which would open the pupil's parachute if he failed to do so himself. Not all pupils achieved instant stability. 'You don't need an altimeter. You need a bloody rev counter,' an instructor was heard to remark to a hapless PJI trainee.

The system had subsequently been adapted during the 1970s by the sport parachuting world, in the form of Accelerated Free Fall Training (AFF). This enables complete novices, after requisite ground training, to sample the sensations and exhilaration of free fall by dropping for up to sixty seconds flanked and physically controlled by an instructor on each side. The Falcons, sometimes using the sport parachuting facilities and aircraft of RAFSPA, have themselves introduced several thrill-seekers to free fall in this way. Janet Ellis, co-presenter of 'Blue Peter' in 1984, was one of the Team's prettier pupils. She was also one of the bravest. Making an introductory static-line descent from the PTS balloon, she broke her hip, but was back at the end of the season to complete her free fall training and make her first AFF descent from a Hercules. She returned the following year to beat the Blue Peter record for a high altitude descent set by John Noakes with the Falcons in the 1970s, at 25,000 feet. At the time of writing, Stuart Miles is preparing to become the third Blue Peter presenter to jump with the Team.

In 1986, the long-established relationship between Falcons and Red Arrows was enhanced by an exchange of 'sensations'. Falcons flew in the back seats of the Arrow's Hawks, and Red Arrow pilots Squadron Leader Gordon Hannam and Flight Lieutenant Tony Lunnon-Wood made AFF descents from 12,000 feet.

'One of the most incredible experiences of my life,' said Tony Lunnon-Wood. 'I may have looked the part outside, but inside there was a quivering jelly.'

Mutually impressed, Falcons and Red Arrows decided that they preferred their own way of presenting the Royal Air Force to the public.

Instant free fall experience is also available now through 'Tandem Jumping', in which the pupil is physically attached to the harness of a qualified tandem master for free fall under a stabilising drogue, and subsequent descent under an enlarged canopy.

The Blue Peter jumps of course attracted favourable publicity, as have various endeavours of the Falcons to associate themselves with selected charities. Fund raising on a minor scale, appearances at charitable functions, and 'training jumps' into local charity galas have long featured in the Falcons itinerary. In 1987 Team leader Ric Allison targeted a major charity - Child Line - for Falcons support. Through advertising consultant Sydney Pemberton a competition for a trip for four to Disneyland, courtesy of TWA, was launched. The competition was free, and all that was asked on the half-a-million leaflets that the Falcons distributed at their shows that season was that a donation be sent direct to Child Line with the entry. Aproximately £15,000 was amassed. It would have been a lot more had RAF regulations allowed the Team actually to collect the donations on the showgrounds. In return, Falcons received valuable publicity through Esther Ranzen's 'That's Life' programme, which for a while screened its opening credits against a film of team members free falling with individual letter-banners spelling out 'That's Life'. At least, it spelt 'That's Life' when they got into the right place in the line-up.

It was a good choice of charity, for Falcons always have had a soft spot for kids. They give frequent presentations, talks, and training jumps at schools, and youngsters make up a large and certainly the most vociferous part of their audiences. Ric Allison remembers how, when the Team was jumping into the Bulawayo Trade Fair in Zimbabwe, it was the kids who made it all worthwhile. It was an interesting but not altogether happy trip. There was administrative hassle. There was Ric being floored by the blunt end of a rifle wielded by the Presidential Guard when he wandered unannounced into the Presidential presence. There was the racial prejudice directed towards Falcons Ken De Souza of Indian parentage and Trinidadian Roger Huskisson. But the children were marvellous. Nothing could restrain them. After each of the four jumps they broke through the police cordons to sweep over the parachutists and their equipment like a grinning black tide. But each time, when the police had cleared them, not one

item of kit was missing.

And there had been one particular child in 1984 … It was in Portugal, where the Falcons had replaced the Red Arrows at the Portuguese National Day celebrations in Lisbon. After an impressive jump from 12,000 feet into a park in the centre of the city, the Team lined up to be presented to the Prime Minister of Portugal and the British Ambassador. As Team Leader Dave Griffith was about to begin the introductions, a Portuguese rushed from the crowd and thrust his baby son between Dave and the Prime Minister, shouting 'Please Mister Falcon, kissa the baby', which, to avoid embarrassment, Dave duly did. He then took the proud father along the line with the two VIPs so that the rest of the Team could kiss the baby too, as well as shake hands with the Prime Minister.

It is from the children that the most pertinent questions come, usually during the many visits to Primary schools carried out by individual Team members, and often prompted by unshakeable logic and an inherent curiosity about the potential for disaster. 'If your main parachute doesn't open, what happens if the reserve parachute fails as well?' asked one nine-year old.

'The reserve never fails,' came the prompt and cosmetic reply.

'Then why don't you use it first …?'

'Next question …?'

After a period during the mid 1980s when Defence economies and other demands on aircraft had restricted the frequency of overseas displays, towards the end of the decade Falcons began to move back onto the international stage. 1987 saw them in Sweden, Italy, France, Belgium

Above: San Diego's Jack Murphy stadium provides a regular setting for an annual Falcon display.

and for the first times in Mexico and Zimbabwe. In 1988 they toured the world. In Australia for the Bi-Centenary celebrations they made a highly publicised descent against the magnificent backdrop of Sydney Bridge and the Opera House, then appeared three times at the Richmond Airshow close to Sydney before audiences of half a million. They moved on to the USA for a jump at San Diego and three drops into the prestigious Harrisburg Airshow, Pennsylvania. In 1989 it was Zimbabwe again. In 1990 it was Singapore. Frequency of shows peaked at 106 completed in 1988. Safety standards peaked the following year when out of 3099 training and display jumps logged by the Falcons there were no parachute malfunctions, no injuries.

In 1990 the Falcons threw a party for all past and present members to mark the 25th anniversary of the Team. Actually, some of us could have reminded them that it was the 29th anniversary, for the Team had formed in 1961. All that happened in 1965 was that they named it after a bird, but we weren't about to spoil the excuse for a good party. And we kept quiet about two-man baton passes, for they marked the year with a 25-man link of Falcons and other PJI free-fallers over El Centro. Also to mark the anniversary, Chris Heathershaw chose a particularly ambitious 'Press Day'. This had long been an annual event, intended to attract media coverage at the beginning of each season. For 1990 the chosen venue was The Tower Of London - an ambitious drop zone for the first display of the year, with only the moat to land in. Or the Thames. On the day, it was raining on

London with a cloud base of 2,000 feet, below the minimum drop height of 2,200. Then the aircraft became unserviceable. But the Chief of the Air Staff and an impressive array of pressmen and cameras were gathered in the moat, so another Hercules was prepared, and London Air Traffic Control agreed to a revised drop time. There remained the problem of the cloud. Skimming its base, the Hercules was flown up the Thames, then at the last moment was banked into a climbing left turn into the cloud to put it on the right track. As the London landscape disappeared under a swirl of grey, Chris gave the signal to jump. Twelve relieved Falcons landed in the moat, trying to look more nonchalant than they felt.

1990 brought another major advance in technique. Sonic Communications provided the Team, without charge, with miniature radios that comprised earphones to be fitted inside the helmet, and throat microphones for those who needed them - namely Team Coach, his number six jumper, and the DZ Sergeant. Their immediate application was to the communication of wind speeds to all members of the Team by the DZ Sergeant. The radios were then applied to a major refinement of the canopy-stack. The Team Coach could now call for synchronised operation of smoke canisters under the canopy, and guide the stack by voice as well as by his own movement. The result was a far quicker and smoother response. Moreover, he could now lead the Team into choreographed aerobatics under their flying wings. After checking with his number six at the centre of the Team that the stack was in good shape, at his word of command the stack would split, the lower six men spiralling out to the right, the upper six peeling away to the

left, all twelve coming together again, pulling the swirls of smoke into single line once more. The stack spiral had become a split spiral.

As with most technical innovations there were minor problems with the radio link. On one occasion the Team radio frequency happened to be that used by a local taxi firm. The Team Coach's exhortations to 'Turn left … Turn left …!' followed almost immediately by a 'Turn right … Turn right …!' threw the city's taxi drivers into confusion. Then there was the display at Eastbourne when the Team Coach asked the DZ party if they could get a wind-reading from the top of a nearby hotel, for close to the sea on a warm day those 200-foot winds can do strange things. Later, the Coach called over the Sonic, 'What's the wind doing then, Denis?'

'Nil winds … nil winds …!' came the immediate response.

'You sure?'

'Yeah. But then I'm still in the lift.'

In 1991 came another major advance. The Falcons donned new parachutes, when the Strato Clouds became due for replacement after six years of excellent service. This time there was no argument over their successor. Display and sport-parachuting experience within PTS wanted Glidepath International's 'Fury', and the Fury they got - a fast nine-cell parachute, stable and reliable, ideal for backing out those stronger winds although hard to rein in when there were no winds at all. And those stronger winds could be faced with more confidence now, for in the event of a malfunction of the main canopy, it now had a square reserve as a back up.

At last, the Falcons had gone *completely* square …

CHAPTER FIVE

FALCONS TODAY

Today's young Falcons demonstrate a level of aerial skill in free fall and under the canopy which for 'Falcon Fathers' had been the stuff of extravagant dreams. Such precision of body flight ... teamwork ... artistry under the canopy ... consistent accuracy on such tiny drop zones.

The advances in performance are perhaps the inevitable products of improvements to equipment, learning opportunities, and training systems, but they are above all due to the enthusiasm and dedication with which these improvements have been pursued and applied by a succession of Team Leaders, Team members, and above all by those wise and masterful Team Coaches: Terry Allen, Doug Peacock, Andy Sweeney, David Ross, Joe France, Bob Souter, Ali McDonald, Ty Barraclough, Brian McGill,

Phil Kelly, Rex Pritchard, Dave Hart....

Far more skillful, more professional in their approach than their founders, today's Falcons are nevertheless of the same breed of spirited young men. Go into the Falcons crew-room today, close your eyes so that you can't see the enlarged photographs on the wall of 25-man links and of square canopies stacked one upon the other, and you could be listening to Snowy Robertson and Jake McLoughlin and Doug Peacock and Tommy Maloney and Johnny Thirtle and any of those who followed 'The Big Six'.

Sit in on a debrief after a recent show ... 'Martin,' says the Team Leader, 'What was your impression of the show?'

'Sir,' comes the deadpan response, 'I don't do impressions. I'm a professional parachutist.'

'Today's young Falcons demonstrate a level of skill which for 'Falcon Fathers' had been the stuff of extravagant dreams.'

They haven't changed. Same dry humour. Same easy camaraderie of shared adventure. Same satisfaction of doing a job they love. Same grumbles when the wind or the cloud base say that they can't do it on this particular day.

They come from the same background as we did, too. Falcons are still drawn from the Physical Education Branch of the Royal Air Force, all highly qualified in the administration and application of the Service's physical training, outdoor activities, resource-and-initiative, rehabilitation, and sporting programmes. They have trained as Parachute Jumping Instructors as one of the advanced specialisations open to officers and NCOs within the trade. The brevet of the PJI is not awarded lightly. Three months of demanding training, searching examination in theory and practice, and a period of probation must be completed satisfactorily before a man is entrusted with the lives of others. When qualified, they join the staff of No 1 Parachute Training School at RAF Brize Norton.

The role of PTS has not changed since Louis Strange formed the unit at Ringway in 1940: teaching Britain's airborne forces to go to war, by parachute.

Techniques and equipment have advanced, but although free fall parachuting features to an increasing extent in the PTS programme, teaching troops to parachute 'en masse', with equipment, by day or night, using static-line operated 'chutes from low altitude, remains the basic trade of the School. Each year it's Static-Line Training Squadron trains some 1600 men of the Parachute Regiment, Special Air Service, Royal Marines, and RAF Regiment. The role of the PJI within the Squadron is to lead his own 'stick' of eight trainees through a progressive

Above: The basic trade of the PJI is to train Britain's airborne forces to go to war, by parachute. Former Falcon Ken D'Souza prepares paratroopers at Aldershot for a training descent ...

Right: ... before despatching them from the Hercules over Hankley Common.

course of ground training; then prepare them for and supervise the eight jumps they need to qualify for coveted airborne wings. The role of the officer PJI is primarily administrative and

within PTS. The primary task of Free Fall Training Squadron is to teach military personnel to free fall in close groups, with equipment, from heights up to 25,000 feet, at night and in demanding weather conditions. It also qualifies PJIs to carry out this highly specialised instruction. The Squadron also has an Adventurous Training Flight which conducts basic and advanced courses in sport parachuting for members of all three Services, supported by its own civil-registered aircraft. And Free Fall Training Squadron commands the Falcons.

Having conducted basic static-line and free fall training for airborne forces, PTS then gives continuation training and operational support for those units through Detachments of PJIs to the Parachute Regiment and to Special Forces. PJIs also provide a nucleus of highly qualified test-jumpers for trials on parachuting equipment and procedures at A & AEE Boscombe Down, the Royal Aircraft Establishment Farnborough, and the Joint Air Transport Establishment at Brize Norton.

From this pool of parachuting expertise are drawn the young Falcons - usually whilst serving their basic trade in Static-Line Training Squadron. They will have shown an early enthusiasm and aptitude for free fall, but this alone is not enough. The personal qualities that a man brings to the Team are as important as his technical skills. An unselfish ability to work as part of a team, and an acceptance of rank without it being a bar to friendship are essential. It's best to be in the company of friends when you're falling together at 120 mph, or trying to ease your canopy into the 'stack' at 2,000 feet. The bearing of the Falcon outside the confines of the Team is important too. He is going to be an

supervisory, and where appropriate to lead by example.

Free fall training has, since its introduction in 1960, expanded to similar Squadron status

Above: Round Britain's coastline with the Falcons. Lyme Regis ...   ... Lundy

ambassador, representing the Royal Air Force and sometimes his country to an international public. Nor will he do this from a smiling distance. On the showgrounds of the world he will be meeting people, shaking their hands, answering their questions, signing autographs for their children. He will attend official receptions. He will give presentations at schools and charity functions and old folk's homes. He will talk to reporters and journalists, speak on radio, appear on television. He will be chosen accordingly.

If he is an officer, he will serve one year as Team Manager, a second as Deputy Leader, a third as Leader. It will require administrative and leadership skills of the highest order as well as free fall talent, and in return will provide him with the most memorable three years of his Service career. If he is a sergeant he will spend his three years as a jumping member, progressing to the more responsible slots in the free fall pattern and the canopy stack as his skills improve, possibly becoming cameraman. The Team Coach - a Flight Sergeant - is probably the only one to have served a previous tour as a Falcon. His experience is immense, his control of his sergeants absolute, and his service to his Team Leader a combination of fatherly advice and diplomatic suggestion.

Our Falcon - if married, and most are - will

... Aberdeen

... Plymouth. (Photo by John Lyne for The Western Morning News)

need an understanding wife. She and the kids won't see much of him during the next three summers, certainly not at weekends. Not to be outdone, several wives of today's Falcons have followed their husbands into the sky, by jumping at Weston-on-the-Green with the RAF Sport Parachute Association.

Women free fallers? Of course. 'So why are there no women in the Team?' some may ask - particularly if they have seen the Red Devils perform, for the Parachute Regiment team long ago applied the old show-jumping maxim that the prettier the face that is put at apparent risk, the bigger the crowds. However, good looks alone have never gained a girl a place amongst

the Devils. The first of them - Jackie Smith, who married one of the Team to become Jackie Young - remains the most successful British competition jumper ever, winning gold for accuracy in the 1978 World Championships with a still unequalled score of ten consecutive dead-centre landings. The girls who have followed her as Red Devils have also earned their places by merit, and have undoubtedly added to the appeal of the team. So why no female Falcons? The Red Devils, being a self-supporting Regimental team, can within reason select members as they wish. Every Falcon, however, is by qualification and trade a PJI, whose job before and after his tour as a professional show jumper is training

paratroopers, then man-handling them and their 100-lb equipment containers in a lurching, low flying Hercules before assisting them into the slipstream. Although the specialisation of PJI is open to WRAF Physical Training Instructors, the physical demands of the job have proved too much for those who have tried it. Perhaps one day ...

Having been selected, our fledgling Falcon will undergo intensive training at the autumn overseas session, usually at El Centro. This will concentrate on bringing his individual techniques to high standard: the precise skills of body-flight needed to form and maintain a link with others; his tracking ability; his awareness of position over the ground and in relation to others in free fall; the increasingly demanding skills of canopy control as one of a team; individual accuracy on the target. In early spring these individual techniques will be applied to Team display procedures in another concentrated period of pre-season training. Further training throughout his three years as a Falcon will also provide the qualification of a military free fall instructor - the QFFI category.

Traditionally, the overseas detachments for intensive training have sought the desert. Since 1977, the desert has been provided by Southern California. There, hosted by the United States Naval Air Facility at El Centro, operating from a desert airstrip onto an adjacent DZ, supported by its RAF Hercules, the Team will concentrate more than fifty jumps for each man into less than

Left: Rex Pritchard - one of a long line of Team Coaches who have been the backbone of Falcons achievement - takes to the air before the accident in 1994 that would have crippled a lesser man.

three weeks of training. Often, Falcons training will be combined with a similar intensity of trials work and basic military free fall carried out by other PJIs. When El Centro has not been available for these essential concentrations of practice, Cyprus or the French Parachute School at Pau have provided the clear skies and the favourable winds.

By the time he takes to the air for his first official display of the season, our young Falcon has learnt to apply his individual skills to the basic components of Team display - team tracking, group relative work, and precision opening in free fall; canopy formation-flying and grouped landings under the opened parachute. He will be proficient in all three types of Falcon presentation. Since the days of 'The Big Six', free fall display has been based on some variation of the 'bomb-burst', designed to illustrate movement across the sky, and adapted to altitude as necessary. Today, three distinct free fall patterns are offered …

When skies are clear enough for a drop from between 8,000 and 12,000 feet, the High Show is presented. The first four men dive from the ramp of the aircraft to form a linked base. Those who follow form two teams of four trackers, each foursome diving outwards from the central base, then swooping back towards it, their smoke trails curving through the sky to demonstrate man's ability to fly in free fall.

If cloud or other circumstances limit the drop to heights from between 4,500 and 8,000 feet, the Mid Show comprises a 4-man group followed closely by linked pairs, the whole Team splitting outwards before they reach opening height to create the bomb-burst.

For those dreadful days when cloud forces the Falcons below 4,500 feet and perhaps as low as their minimum drop height of 2,200, the Team exits for a Low Show in two simultaneous 'sticks' of six, each stick diving away from the other to ensure safe separation for opening their 'chutes.

Whatever the duration and pattern of free fall display, it will put the Team into a position from which it can attain the drop zone, and in so doing can also display canopy aerobatics - the stack, the spiral, and now the split stack. And at the end of it - that impressive succession of smoky landings on the two tiny target crosses.

A variety of aircraft have launched the Team on their shows. Today the C130 Hercules remains the favoured jump-ship, with its roomy rear door so ideal for mass departures, and its two side doors offering an alternative means of exit. For reasons of economy in fuel and flying hours, or because it is urgently required elsewhere - the Falklands and Gulf wars, or Bosnian emergencies for example - the Hercules has not always been available. Its place has then been taken by Andovers, or by helicopters.

The smaller Andover offers less elbow room for exits, but has the advantage of being more responsive to those last-second corrections from the 'spotter' as he tries to bring it overhead the calculated release point. The crews of Northolt-based No 32 Squadron who fly the Andovers are more accustomed to flying VIPs than PJIs, but adjusted early to the task, just as the PJIs adjusted to the trays of cling-filmed crustless sandwiches which they were offered on one flight instead of the standard white 'butty box'.

Falcons first used helicopters for display in Hong Kong in 1971, and it may be thought that their hover capability provides an ideal jumping platform. However, although leaping into still air is a pleasant sensation, it is a precarious one. A free-faller needs air pressure to work with, and unless this is provided by the forward momentum of the machine from which he jumps, he must waffle around for a few seconds until his own gathering speed creates it. So for display drops the Puma and Chinook helicopters occasionally used by the Falcons today are flown at some 70 mph.

Whatever the type of aircraft, one thing has remained constant: the outstanding co-operation and skills offered so generously by their crews. The bond between dropper and dropped has been an essential factor in the success of Falcons displays since John Leary and John Taylor delivered us with such professional aplomb and - in hindsight - with such astounding accuracy over Farnborough in 1961. Those high standards have been maintained to this day, much assisted by the practice of assigning specific crews to the support of the Falcons during each season - not their only task, of course, for just as Falcons are primarily PJIs with an operational training role, so those who deliver them are first and foremost operational pilots.

Other areas of support have not always attracted such mutual respect, but happily the traditional discords have greatly diminished - particularly that between the Falcons and the procurement agencies and engineering branches

The training of military free fallers to drop from high altitude and at night if necessary, carrying weapons, equipment, and personal oxygen supply, will be the role of the Falcon after his three years on the showgrounds of the world. (Photo by Alistair Wright for The Military Picture Library)

who approve and provide their equipment. It is today unlikely that the PJI will be credited by 'authority' with so little practical and technical intelligence - as we were in 1961. It is today unlikely that a Falcon will have to come close to killing himself before a long-overdue modification is approved - as Pete McCumiskey did in 1963. It is unlikely that a Team Leader will have to refuse to ask the Team to jump with an obviously unsafe type of parachute before it is replaced - as Mike Milburn did in 1984.

At operational level, the support of the Survival Equipment Fitters who have become integrated members of the Team always has contributed immeasurably to the outstanding record of safety. In over 30 years of display jumping no Falcon has died as a result of a parachuting accident, none injured beyond repair. Accidents happen. Those night descents from high altitude, with oxygen kit and full military equipment that all Falcons carry out to gain their Military Free Fall Instructor category, have never been popular. Team Leader Rhys Cowsill led one such 'patrol' from 18,000 feet whilst training at El Centro. Those ghosting down above him heard Rhys hit and curse and bounce along the ground. 'You okay, boss?' one called through the darkness after landing.

'Yeah. For a minute I thought I'd broke my effing leg...'

After clearing the DZ it was discovered that he *had* broken his effing leg.

Team Coach Rex Pritchard was even more unlucky. Leading the 1994 Falcons into their first display of the year, an almost impossible combination of surface turbulence and down-draught collapsed his canopy, hurled him into the ground from some hundred feet, and shattered his right leg. Outstanding surgery at Oxford's John Radcliffe Hospital rebuilt him, and outstanding willpower has - almost a year later - brought Rex back to parachuting, against all expectation.

Yes, accidents happen. But Falcons sustain more injuries on the sports field than on their drop zones. The aim that was established in 1961 of taking the dicing-with-death label from around the neck of parachuting has been achieved, without lessening the drama. The tantalising aura of high risk is still there, but the risk is under control: it is spectacular skill that the Falcon seeks to display, not a life in danger. Welcomed by today's Falcons is an easing of the Ministry of Defence regulations that have previously frowned so sternly upon commercial enterprise and sponsorship within the Service. The initiatives of individual Team Leaders during the 1980s and in particular Ric Allison's involvement with the Child Line charity illustrated the marketing potential of the Team at a time when attitudes towards commercial association were beginning to soften. The prominent association of the 1994 Falcons with Children In Need again provided funds for a deserving charity, and a valuable public-relations exercise for the Royal Air Force.

The material support that the Team now enjoys from commercial companies such as Sonic Communications, Colab Photo Labs, Panasonic, Sony, Minolta Cameras, Fuji Films, Mercury Paging, Forte Hotels and Pennine Communications in return for no more than grateful acknowledgement in the Falcons annual brochure points the way towards major commercial sponsorship, within the necessary guidelines prescribed by MOD. In return for tasteful advertising through their association with the Falcons such a sponsor might give material support for the Team in the form of ancillary equipment; might indirectly benefit Service charities; might provide additional professional publicity.

The annual programme of displays is based on bids submitted by show organisers to the MOD Participation Committee. Team management advises on the suitability of DZs and on pertinent administrative and technical considerations, and a final programme is agreed. In the past, opportunites to promote the Falcons within the general body of national and international show promoters and to present the Team and the RAF to a larger public have been lost. An invitation from the BBC in 1986 for the Falcons to participate in the coverage of the Royal Wedding of Prince Andrew and Sarah Ferguson was turned down by MOD, as was an invitation to jump at the Commonwealth Games that same year. The Falcons' own frustrations were compounded when the Red Devils readily accepted the former, and the Royal Marines Parachute Display Team appeared at the latter. The signs are that such golden opportunites would not be missed again, and that there is now a more energetic and imaginative promotion of the Falcons before they ever get into the sky: once there, they can speak for themselves most eloquently.

What of the future? Inevitably, the very existence of the Falcons comes under close scrutiny with every Defence Review. Were they no more than professional show jumpers, despite their relatively low cost as a showcase for the spirit and skills of the Service, and despite the Team's value to the RAF Public Relations and Recruiting campaigns, it is unlikely that the team would have survived the more drastic cuts in defence expenditure during the thirty years of their history - and particularly the most recent. The ultimate justification for the Falcons lies in the carry-over value of the training they undergo, the techniques and equipment they help to develop, and the example of parachuting excellence they portray - all of which have direct application to the training of Britain's airborne forces for war.

Their public-relations impact on an international audience is less easily quantified, but the 1994 season gave an outstanding example of it. In Berlin the Team jumped into the last Queen's Birthday Parade to be held in the city. As they afterwards mingled with the crowd, it was they and not the Senior Officers in the VIP enclosure nor the troops on parade who received the handshakes and the pats on the back and the sometimes tearful thanks for 50 years of Allied guardianship. This accessibility of impressive young servicemen to an impressed public is a unique asset, which cannot be priced. Evaluators of military worth normally dislike abstract qualities. How gratifying, therefore, that the abstract qualities of the Falcons have survived and flourished for 35 years of Defence Reviews. And what will they make of this recently confirmed future? Although it is difficult to see how, techniques and equipment will continue to improve, for parachutists by their very nature are constantly seeking advance, innovation, novelty. Parachutes will get better. DZs will get tighter and more imaginative. New and more precise smoke-patterns will be drawn in the sky in free fall and particularly under the

Above: And as for the Falcon himself, little has changed. As Snowy Robertson said at the founding of the Team in 1961, 'Where else would I get paid for having such a good time?'

Right: Snowy Robertson.

canopies. And hopefully the management and presentation of these talents will keep pace with them.

The only thing that will surely not change is the nature of the man. When someone in those crowds who so loudly applaud the Falcons as they come swooping down out of the skies subsequently asks of a smiling young man wearing blue overalls that still smell of smoke and bear the brevet of the PJI and the emblem of a bird of prey, 'Why do you do it?', today's Falcon will still grin as Snowy Robertson used to grin and say as he used to say, 'Where else would I get paid for having such a good time?'

HOW SONIC WORKS

A Sonic radio is used to pass wind measurements and other essential information to the Falcons, (above) who are all equipped with helmet-receivers. Team Leader (above right) and Team Coach, using Sonic boom microphone, can also transmit instructions to the Team - particularly useful for directing manoeuvres during canopy flight.

The Team cameraman wears helmet-mounted video and stills cameras on all descents. Video film can be recorded or transmitted live to the ground (above) using a Sonic Air-to-Ground Microwave system. Video film is used extensively for de-briefing individual members of the Team.

THE FALCONS ROLL-CALL

Note: Until 1970, the hard core of regular display jumpers were supplemented on an availability basis from the pool of other free fallers at No 1 PTS, hence the seemingly larger 'teams' of the early 60s.

1959

Not yet an authorised team, the following represented the Royal Air Force in major displays in Australia and/or New Zealand:

Flt Lt   Peter Hearn
Fg Off   John Thirtle
Sgt   Alf Card
Sgt   Tommy Maloney
Sgt   Keith Teesdale
Sgt   Peter Denley
Sgt   Snowy Robertson
Sgt   Russell Nicholas

1961

Flt Lt   Peter Hearn
Flt Lt   John Thirtle
Sgt   Tommy Maloney
Sgt   Snowy Robertson
Sgt   Doug Peacock
Sgt   Jake McLoughlin

1962

Flt Lt   Peter Hearn
Flt Lt   Peter Williams
Flt Lt   Peter McCumiskey
Sgt   Doug Peacock
Sgt   Brian Jones
Sgt   Stan Phipps
Sgt   Mick Torrevill
Sgt   Tony Charlton
Sgt   Snowy Robertson
Sgt   Paul Hewitt
Sgt   Dave Francombe
Sgt   Norman Hoffman

1963

Flt Lt   Peter McCumiskey
Flt Lt   Bert Shearer
Sgt   Ken Kidd
Sgt   Doug Peacock
Sgt   Dave Francombe
Sgt   Paul Hewitt
Sgt   Norman Pilling
Sgt   Tony Charlton
Sgt   Norman Hoffman
Sgt   Brian Clark-Sutton
Sgt   Mick Torrevill

1964

Flt Lt   Peter Williams
Flt Lt   John Thirtle
FS   Brian Hedley
Sgt   Ron Mitchell
Sgt   Brian Jones
Sgt   Norman Hoffman
Sgt   Jan Sparkes
Sgt   Paul Hewitt
Sgt   Dave Francombe
Sgt   Pete McCrink
Sgt   Tony Charlton
Sgt   Brian Clark-Sutton
Sgt   Julian Tasker
Sgt   Ray Brettell

1965

Flt Lt   John Thirtle
Flt Lt   Stuart Cameron
Flt Lt   Bert Shearer
FS   Terry Allen
Sgt   Ray Brettell
Sgt   Ron Mitchell
Sgt   Alan Burdett
Sgt   Tony Charlton
Sgt   Brian Clark-Sutton
Sgt   William Cook
Sgt   Tony De Cadiz
Sgt   Gordon Flint
Sgt   Dave Francombe
Sgt   Mick Geelan
Sgt   Paul Hewitt
Sgt   Ken Jacobs
Sgt   David Jones
Sgt   Ken Mapplebeck
Sgt   Pete McCrink
Sgt   Norman Pilling
Sgt   Snowy Robertson
Sgt   Julian Tasker
Sgt   Jan Sparkes

1966

Flt Lt   Stuart Cameron
Flt Lt   Bert Shearer
Flt Lt   Les Evans
FS   Terry Allen
Sgt   Pete McCrink
Sgt   Ron Mitchell
Sgt   Mick Geelan
Sgt   Brian Jones
Sgt   Paul Hewitt
Sgt   Jan Sparkes
Sgt   Tony De Cadiz
Sgt   Ken Mapplebeck
Sgt   David Jones
Sgt   Alan Burdett
Sgt   Dave Francombe
Sgt   Brian Clark-Sutton
Sgt   Snowy Robertson

1967

Flt Lt   Stuart Cameron
Flt Lt   Les Evans
Flt Lt   Brian Hedley
Fg Off   Geoff Greenland
FS   Terry Allen
Sgt   Tony Charlton
Sgt   Julien Tasker
Sgt   Brian Clark-Sutton
Sgt   David Jones
Sgt   Doug Peacock
Sgt   Andy Sweeney
Sgt   George Muir
Sgt   Ray Brettel
Sgt   Ken Mapplebeck
Sgt   Pete George
Sgt   William Cook

1968

Fg Off   Geoff Greenland
Flt Lt   Mervyn Green
Fg Off   Brian Hedley
FS   Terry Allen
FS   Tony Charlton
FS   Julien Tasker
Sgt   Doug Peacock
Sgt   Ken Mapplebeck
Sgt   Pete Davis
Sgt   Andy Sweeney
Sgt   Pete George
Sgt   Ray Brettel
Sgt   George Muir
Sgt   David Jones
Sgt   Allan Rhind
Sgt   Ed Mallinson
Sgt   George Featherstone

1969

Flt Lt   Mervyn Green
Fg Off   David Cobb
FS   Terry Allen
Sgt   Allan Rhind
Sgt   Ed Mallinson
Sgt   Pete George
Sgt   Les Allworthy
Sgt   Gordon Flint
Sgt   Pete Davis

Sgt   David Jones
Sgt   Alan Burdett
Sgt   Dave Francombe
Sgt   Brian Clark-Sutton
Sgt   Snowy Robertson

1970

Flt Lt   David Cobb
Fg Off   Alan Jones
FS   Doug Peacock
Sgt   Sid Garrard
Sgt   George Featherstone
Sgt   Pete George
Sgt   Les Allworthy
Sgt   George Long
Sgt   Barry Furness
Sgt   William Cook
Sgt   David Ross

1971

Flt Lt   Alan Jones
Flt Lt   Gwynne Morgan
Fg Off   John Parry
FS   Doug Peacock
Sgt   Allan Rhind
Sgt   Doug Dewar
Sgt   David Ross
Sgt   Snowy Robertson
Sgt   George Featherstone
Sgt   Bob Souter
Sgt   Ian Harper
Sgt   Ray Willis
Sgt   Sid Garrard
Sgt   Henry MacDonald
Sgt   Harry Parkinson

1972

Flt Lt   Gwynne Morgan
Flt Lt   Alec Jackson
Flt Lt   Paul Millard
FS   Andy Sweeney
Sgt   Henry MacDonald
Sgt   Bob Souter
Sgt   Ray Willis
Sgt   David Ross
Sgt   Colin Blythe
Sgt   Ty Barraclough
Sgt   Joe France
Sgt   Doug Fletcher
Sgt   Harry Parkinson

1973

Flt Lt   Alec Jackson
Flt Lt   Johnny Johnston

Sgt   David Jones
Sgt   Alan Burdett
Sgt   Dave Francombe
Sgt   Brian Clark-Sutton
Sgt   Snowy Robertson

Sgt   Doug Dewar
Sgt   George Featherstone
Sgt   David Ross
Sgt   Sid Garrard

Flt Lt   John Grimes
FS   Andy Sweeney
Sgt   Ray Willis
Sgt   Bob Souter
Sgt   Dennis Wreford
Sgt   Colin Blythe
Sgt   Terry Keoghan
Sgt   Joe France
Sgt   Ty Barraclough
Sgt   Doug Fletcher
Sgt   Henry MacDonald
Sgt   Chris Buchan

1974

Flt Lt   Johnny Johnston
Fg Off   Peter Watson
Fg Off   Dick Wooding
FS   Andy Sweeney
Sgt   Joe France
Sgt   Ty Barraclough
Sgt   Chris Buchan
Sgt   Terry Cooke
Sgt   Doug Fletcher
Sgt   Jim Graham
Sgt   Bob Kent
Sgt   Terry Keoghan
Sgt   Dennis Wreford
Sgt   Joe Pryce
Sgt   Chris Vipond

1975

Flt Lt   Peter Watson
Flt Lt   Clive Hillman
Fg Off   Paul Rogers
FS   David Ross
Sgt   Ty Barraclough
Sgt   Chris Buchan
Sgt   Terry Cooke
Sgt   Geoff Diggle
Sgt   Jim Graham
Sgt   Bob Kent
Sgt   Steve McBrine
Sgt   Graham Pierce
Sgt   Steve Rowe
Sgt   Joe Pryce
Sgt   Trevor Green

1976

Flt Lt   Clive Hillman
Flt Lt   Simon Bales
Flt Lt   Paul Rogers
FS   David Ross
Sgt   Geoff Diggle

Sgt Jim Graham
Sgt Terry Cooke
Sgt Graham Pierce
Sgt Bob Kent
Sgt Steve Rowe
Sgt Joe McCready
Sgt Dave Armstrong
Sgt Jim Gregor
Sgt Martin Daccus
Sgt Trevor Green

1977

Flt Lt Simon Bales
Flt Lt Roger Nicolle
Flt Lt John Conrad
FS David Ross
Sgt Martin Daccus
Sgt Dave Armstrong
Sgt John Gregor
Sgt Tommy Johnson
Sgt Phil Kelly
Sgt Bob Kent
Sgt Ali MacDonald
Sgt Joe McCready
Sgt Graham Pierce
Sgt Steve Rowe
Sgt Trevor Green

1978

Flt Lt Roger Nicolle
Flt Lt Steve Percival
Flt Lt Bryan Morris
FS Joe France
Sgt Dave Armstrong
Sgt John Gregor
Sgt Joe McCready
Sgt Tommy Johnson
Sgt Phil Kelly
Sgt Ali MacDonald
Sgt Seamus Byrne
Sgt Pete Colley
Sgt Brian Davies
Sgt Miko Mikolajewski
Sgt Al Isted

1979

Flt Lt Peter Smout
Flt Lt Keith Fricker
Flt Lt Bryan Morris
FS Joe France
Sgt Pete Colley
Sgt Brian Davies
Sgt Chris Duerden
Sgt Dave Emerson
Sgt Pat Feeney
Sgt Tommy Johnson
Sgt Phil Kelly
Sgt Ali MacDonald
Sgt Miko Mikolajewski
Sgt Pete Reynolds
Sgt Al Isted

1980

Flt Lt Keith Fricker
Flt Lt Geoff Diggle
Flt Lt Roger Harrison

FS Bob Souter
Sgt Chris Beadel
Sgt Pete Colley
Sgt Brian Davies
Sgt Chris Duerden
Sgt Dave Emerson
Sgt Phil Kelly
Sgt Miko Mikolajewski
Sgt Pete Reynolds
Sgt Pat Feeney
Sgt Steve Tansley
Sgt Ken Haines

1981

Flt Lt Geoff Diggle
Flt Lt Ian Gardiner
Flt Lt Brian Stevenson
FS Bob Souter
Sgt Chris Duerden
Sgt Pat Feeney
Sgt Pete Reynolds
Sgt Chris Beadel
Sgt Dave Emerson
Sgt Allyn Davies
Sgt Steve Tansley
Sgt Dave Wood
Sgt Dave Hart
Sgt Bob Webb
Sgt Brian Hill

1982

Flt Lt Ian Gardiner
Flt Lt Duncan Layfield
Flt Lt Brian Stevenson
FS Bob Souter
Sgt Chris Beadel
Sgt Steve Tansley
Sgt Pat Feeney
Sgt Allyn Davies
Sgt Bob Webb
Sgt Dave Wood
Sgt Dave Hart
Sgt Rex Pritchard
Sgt Nigel Rogoff
Sgt Jim Hughes
Sgt Brian Hill

1983

Flt Lt Brian Stevenson
Flt Lt Dave Griffiths
Flt Lt Mike Milburn
FS Ali MacDonald
Sgt Dave Wood
Sgt Bob Webb
Sgt Dave Hart
Sgt Allyn Davies
Sgt Rex Pritchard
Sgt Nigel Rogoff
Sgt Jim Hughes
Sgt Rod Crawford
Sgt Simon Perry
Sgt Nick Oswald
Sgt Al Chaney

1984

Flt Lt Dave Griffiths
Flt Lt Mike Milburn

Flt Lt Derek Warby
FS Ali MacDonald
Sgt Rex Pritchard
Sgt Nigel Rogoff
Sgt Jim Hughes
Sgt Rod Crawford
Sgt Simon Perry
Sgt Nick Oswald
Sgt Barry Charnock
Sgt Mark Petty
Sgt Reg Bailey
Sgt Andy Stalker
Sgt Doug Brown

1985

Flt Lt Mike Milburn
Flt Lt Derek Warby
Flt Lt Ric Allison
FS Ty Barraclough
Sgt Rod Crawford
Sgt Simon Perry
Sgt Nick Oswald
Sgt Barry Charnock
Sgt Mark Perry
Sgt Andy Stalker
Sgt Chris Francis
Sgt Nick Martin
Sgt Ken D'Souza
Sgt Roger Huskisson
Sgt Doug Brown

1986

Flt Lt Derek Warby
Flt Lt Ric Allison
Flt Lt Ali Bridle
FS Ty Barraclough
Sgt Barry Charnock
Sgt Mark Perry
Sgt Andy Stalker
Sgt Chris Francis
Sgt Roger Huskisson
Sgt Nick Martin
Sgt Ken D'Souza
Sgt Gordon Bucknall
Sgt Robbie Blain
Sgt Chris Headley
Sgt Doug Brown

1987

Flt Lt Ric Allison
Flt Lt Ali Bridle
Flt Lt Tom Bown
FS Ty Barraclough
Sgt Gordon Bucknall
Sgt Ken D'Souza
Sgt Roger Huskisson
Sgt Robbie Blain
Sgt Chris Headley
Sgt Andy Dearlove
Sgt Pete Charnock
Sgt Charlie Quinn
Sgt Mark Wood
Sgt Ali Wright
Sgt Doug Brown

1988

Flt Lt Ali Bridle
Flt Lt Tom Bown
Flt Lt Glynn Allcock
FS Brian McGill
Sgt Robbie Blain
Sgt Gordon Bucknall
Sgt Chris Headley
Sgt Pete Charnock
Sgt Andy Dearlove
Sgt Mark Wood
Sgt Ali Wright
Sgt Steve Cowell
Sgt Jim Thomas
Sgt Kevin Woolnough
Sgt Andy Bassinder

1989

Flt Lt Tom Bown
Flt Lt Chris Heathershaw
Flt Lt Glynn Allcock
FS Phil Kelly
Sgt Pete Charnock
Sgt Andy Dearlove
Sgt Mark Wood
Sgt Ali Wright
Sgt Steve Cowell
Sgt Jim Thomas
Sgt Kevin Woolnough
Sgt Simon Rushton
Sgt Jimmy Thompson
Sgt Pete Woodward
Sgt Andy Bassinder

1990

Flt Lt Chris Heathershaw
Flt Lt Mark Smith
Flt Lt Howard Marsh
FS Phil Kelly
Sgt Steve Cowell
Sgt Jim Thomas
Sgt Kevin Woolnough
Sgt Simon Rushton
Sgt Jimmy Thompson
Sgt Pete Woodward
Sgt Martin Byrne
Sgt Paul Hunt
Sgt Greg McKenzie
Sgt Graham Roberts
Sgt John Ramsay

1991

Flt Lt Mark Smith
Flt Lt Rhys Cowsill
Flt Lt Howard Marsh
FS Phil Kelly
Sgt Pete Woodward
Sgt Jim Thompson
Sgt Simon Rushton
Sgt Greg McKenzie
Sgt Martin Byrne
Sgt Paul Hunt
Sgt Graham Roberts
Sgt Jack Dilley
Sgt Chris Williams

Sgt Paul Floyd
Sgt Mike Webster

1992

Flt Lt Rhys Cowsill
Flt Lt Alex Jones
Flt Lt Steve Darling
FS Rex Pritchard
Sgt Jack Dilley
Sgt Paul Floyd
Sgt Greg McKenzie
Sgt Martin Byrne
Sgt Steve Tucker
Sgt Graham Roberts
Sgt Chris Williams
Sgt Andy Wright
Sgt Mike Webster

1993

Flt Lt Alex Jones
Flt Lt Steve Darling
Flt Lt Dave Paveley
FS Rex Pritchard
Sgt Martin Byrne
Sgt Jack Dilley
Sgt Chris Williams
Sgt Steve Tucker
Sgt Paul Floyd
Sgt Andy Wright
Sgt Colin Fallows
Sgt Tony Isherwood
Sgt Mike Webster

1994

Flt Lt Steve Darling
Flt Lt Dave Paveley
Flt Lt Alistair Hunt
FS Rex Pritchard
Sgt Andy Wright
Sgt Steve Tucker
Sgt Tony Isherwood
Sgt Colin Fallows
Sgt Mark Probert
Sgt Paul Usherwood
Sgt Neil Dawson
Sgt Ken Peers
Sgt Jed Robinson
Sgt Kev McCrone

1995

Flt Lt Dave Paveley
Flt Lt Alistair Hunt
Flt Lt Martin Jarvis
FS Dave Hart
Sgt Ken Peers
Sgt Nick Brooksbank
Sgt Neil Dawson
Sgt Mark Probert
Sgt Paul Usherwood
Sgt Mark Luffman
Sgt Kev Kinvig
Sgt Jez Towler
Sgt Tim Shepherd
Sgt Colin Whithers
Sgt Dave McCulloch

GLOSSARY

ADVENTURE TRAINING A tri-Service scheme that provides challenging experience for military personnel through a variety of adventure sports, including parachuting.

AFF Accelerated Free Fall. An advanced training system whereby the pupil is physically assisted in free fall by two instructors. A development of the 'buddy system' pioneered in USA in the 1960s.

AIR LOAD MASTER The member of an aircrew on transport aircraft responsible for load and passengers. Sometimes known as 'Loadie'.

BLANK GORE The aperture in a round canopy through which air escapes to give a ram-jet effect, which propels the parachute in the opposite direction.

CRW Canopy Relative Work. The linking of square canopies in various patterns and sequences of pattern during flight.

CONQUISTADOR A refined form of the TU blank-gore parachute, used by the Falcons in the mid-1960s.

CUTAWAY The process whereby a malfunctioned main canopy can be released (cut away) to allow the parachutist to fall free and operate his reserve 'chute, or have it automatically operated.

DZ Dropping Zone - the designated area to which parachutists seek to land.

DUMMY RUN A practice run over the DZ by the dropping aircraft, or a live run that is aborted for any reason.

FURY The most recent square parachute used by the Falcons, made by Glidepath International.

GQ-236 The square parachute used by the Falcons in the 1980s, made by GQ Parachute Company.

GQ-360 The square parachute currently used for military free fall, made by GQ Parachute Company.

OPENING POINT The point on the ground above which free fall parachutists aim to open their parachutes in order to achieve their ground target.

P-HOUR The time at which a parachute drop is planned to commence.

PJI Parachute Jumping Instructor of the RAF.

PTS No. 1 Parachute Training School, a RAF unit called 'No.1' in 1942 to differentiate it from similar Schools established in the Middle East and India.

PC Para-Commander parachute, the ultimate blank-gore design, used by the Falcons in 1960s and '70s.

PIGGYBACK Parachute design combining main and reserve in one back-pack - an advance on the older chest-mounted reserve system.

RAFSPA Royal Air Force Sport Parachute Association - the body that governs sport parachuting in the RAF and provides training under the Adventure Training Scheme.

RELATIVE WORK The combination of free fall skills by two or more parachutists to form links, formations, and sequential formations.

RELEASE POINT The point over the ground at which parachutists are released in order to achieve their opening point.

ROUND PARACHUTE Parachutes that use a traditional circular canopy, with or without blank gores.

RUN-IN TRACK The path that the aircraft takes to achieve the release point. Usually a track that takes it over the ground target, into wind.

SKYDIVING The term coined by sport parachutists in the late 1950s to describe the free fall element of a parachute drop, later applied to the sport as a whole.

SONIC COMMUNICATIONS The in-helmet radio link between individual Falcons and the ground, provided by Sonic Communications International Ltd., who also provide the direct air-to-ground film link.

SPOTTING The process whereby a parachutist (in the case of the Falcons the Team Leader and/or Team Coach) guides the aircraft through its pilot onto the release point.

SQUARE PARACHUTE Parachutes with a ram-air rectangular-shaped canopy, obtaining lift and forward momentum from flow of air.

STACKING The positioning of parachutes in flight one above and slightly behind the other. The stack might for display purposes be 'spiralled' or 'split'.

STATIC LINE As an alternative to manual operation, parachutes may be opened automatically by a length of line attached to the aircraft - the standard method of low level delivery of paratroops. A 'chute designed for this purpose is called a statichute.

STICK A group of parachutists leaving the aircraft one after the other. Two sticks jumping from separate doors are called simultaneous sticks.

STRATO CLOUD The first square parachute used by the Falcons, in the 1970s.

SURVIVAL EQUIPMENT FITTER A RAF tradesman, specialised in the packing and maintenance of parachutes.

TU PARACHUTE A blank-gore parachute of the early 1960s, the blank gore design incorporting two inverted and linked 'T' shapes.

TANDEM JUMPING An advanced free fall training system in which the pupil remains attached to an instructor throughout free fall and under the canopy.

TERMINAL VELOCITY The constant speed that a free-falling body reaches when gravity and air pressure are balanced, averaging 176 fps, approx 120 mph.

TRACKING Movement across the sky in free fall, most effective when the body assumes an aerofoil position.

XL CLOUD Square parachute used by the Falcons during 1980s.